PRAISE FOR *THE FUN FORMULA*

"Joel Comm amazes me with his ability to have success after success. But what's truly incredible is that he makes it look easy! In this book he's reverse-engineered his "fun formula" and made it available for everyone. Read it and prepare to *ignite* your business and your life!"

—**JOHN LEE DUMAS**, host of *Entrepreneurs on Fire* podcast

"Taking risks, following your heart, and trusting the process are major keys to becoming known in a noisy world. Joel Comm has got this formula figured out and makes it simple in this book. Get ready for an enlightening and fun read that can get you closer to living your purpose and experiencing great joy on the journey!"

—**MARK SCHAEFER**, author of *Known*

"Wow, does this book shine the light on a huge issue for us entrepreneurs— the constant hustle—you know what I mean? This book is going to help you reevaluate the hustle and reintroduce *fun* into your life and business. It's a life changer!"

—**KIM GARST**, online business strategist and bestselling author

"The world is noisy, often complicated, and always challenging. Life might not be easy all the time and in this book, Joel Comm reminds us of what's important: to live with a heart-centered approach in all we do; to show up, take shots, and genuinely have fun with how we're living every day of our lives."

—**CHRIS DUCKER**, bestselling author of *Rise of the Youpreneur*

"Life is too short to forget about enjoying the moments. It's so easy to think that we'll start having fun tomorrow or that our next job will give us satisfaction, but we forget the importance of living a fulfilled life. Joel Comm brilliantly pushes us to take risks and embrace not only the possibility but also the reality of a fun, prosperous life now."

—**RACHEL MARIE MARTIN**, author of FindingJoy.net

"Having known Joel Comm for a few years and having worked with him for nearly a year on the *Bad Crypto Podcast*, I can say nobody knows how to make work more fun than Joel Comm. By reading this book you'll get the blueprint on how to turn your passion into profits. You'll also learn how to live more in the present and how to actually have fun building your business empire!"

—**TRAVIS WRIGHT**, author and marketing technologist

"As with all of his ideas, Joel Comm has created something that I'm envious I didn't think of first. This is really worth your time! And it's fun!"

—**CHRIS BROGAN**, *New York Times* bestselling author of *Trust Agents*

"I don't know anyone who squeezes fun out of every situation more than Joel. He walks the walk—and it's a silly one."

—**MICHAEL O'NEAL**, host of *The Solopreneur Hour*

"Joel Comm is a man of many talents. A great entrepreneur, a top social media influencer, an excellent writer, I could go on. But who knew that he also had the ability to tap into the current zeitgeist? At this time of great change and even greater division, what we really need—collectively and individually—is a bit more fun. *The Fun Formula* delivers. Written with wit, insight, intelligence, actionable take-aways, and, yes, fun, it could also easily be called 'The Success Formula' or 'The Life Formula.' Maybe my biggest compliment is this: I wish I had written it!"

—**STEVE STRAUSS**, *USA Today* senior small business columnist and bestselling author of *The Small Business Bible*

"Joel Comm gets it right with this approach to business and life. This book teaches you exactly how to shift your situation to make your work fun again."

—**LEWIS HOWES**, *New York Times* bestselling author of *The School of Greatness*

The Fun Formula

ALSO BY JOEL COMM

The AdSense Code

KaChing

Twitter Power 3.0 (with Dave Taylor)

Self-Employed (with John Rampton)

Live Video Revolution

The Fun Formula

How Curiosity, Risk-Taking, and Serendipity
Can Revolutionize How You Work

JOEL COMM

NELSON
BOOKS

An Imprint of Thomas Nelson

Published in Nashville, Tennessee, by Nelson Books, an imprint of Thomas Nelson. Nelson Books and Thomas Nelson are registered trademarks of HarperCollins Christian Publishing, Inc.

Published in association with the literary agency of Literary Management Group, LLC.

Thomas Nelson titles may be purchased in bulk for educational, business, fund-raising, or sales promotional use. For information, please e-mail SpecialMarkets@ThomasNelson.com.

Scripture quotations are taken from the Holy Bible, New International Version®, NIV®. Copyright © 1973, 1978, 1984, 2011 by Biblica, Inc.® Used by permission of Zondervan. All rights reserved worldwide. www.Zondervan. com. The "NIV" and "New International Version" are trademarks registered in the United States Patent and Trademark Office by Biblica, Inc.®

Any Internet addresses, phone numbers, or company or product information printed in this book are offered as a resource and are not intended in any way to be or to imply an endorsement by Thomas Nelson, nor does Thomas Nelson vouch for the existence, content, or services of these sites, phone numbers, companies, or products beyond the life of this book.

ISBN 978-1-4002-0194-5 (HC)
ISBN 978-1-4002-0195-2 (eBook)
ISBN 978-1-4002-0886-9 (IE)

Library of Congress Control Number: 2018932503

Printed in the United States of America
18 19 20 21 22 LSC 10 9 8 7 6 5 4 3 2 1

This book is dedicated to my dear friend, Mark Jones, who suddenly and unexpectedly went home to be with the Lord as I was putting the finishing touches on this manuscript. While beginning a book titled Fun *on such a somber note may seem unusual, Mark's life was fully lived, and this tragic loss is a reminder that we must indeed* carpe diem.

CONTENTS

CONTENTS

FOREWORD

I still remember not just the day but the moment I first met Joel Comm. It was at a conference in San Diego, at an event for speakers. This man, whom I had never met (or admittedly, even heard of) before, approached me with an extended hand and a smile and said how much he enjoyed and appreciated my work. We instantly bonded (well, at least I did) when he started sharing stories of going to Disneyland when he was five years old and of returning as an "adult." (I intentionally put adult in quotes, because acting like an adult is all relative, isn't it? But I'll get to that in a second.)

We quickly found that we had much more in common than simply being Disney fans. We both had very circuitous journeys and adventures getting from where we started to where we are now. (I was an attorney in New Jersey before following my passion for Disney and moving to Florida.)

The more I learned about Joel, both that evening and over the friendship that grew from it, the more I liked him. He told every story enthusiastically with wide-eyed excitement on his face. And one thing I believe helped create a bond between us was that we were both in the same place. I don't mean in the same business, but in how we went about doing it.

Joel and I both do what we love full-time. It's not just our job or business—it's our lifestyle. It's our passion. It's our philosophy. It's who we are. But more importantly, we don't just have the privilege, blessing, and ability to do what we love and have our passion be our profession, but we have fun while doing it.

Over time, I have come to learn that such a feeling in one's job, and sometimes even in one's daily life, is not as common as it should be.

So how do you start down the path toward living a life that is fun? Well, I think you are well on your way simply because you're holding Joel's book in your hand, and I hope you will take inspiration from him. Enjoying a life that is both fun and rewarding doesn't happen overnight. But ask yourself if what you are doing today is getting you closer to where you want to be tomorrow. Then start taking small steps every day.

Happiness and fun should be a way of life, not a destination. Find and savor it along the way, not at the end of the road.

You can't fake it in audio or video, and when I watch and listen to Joel, I can tell that he "walks the walk" and is having fun doing what he does. Let him and this book serve as guides to help you find and create your own happy ending and enjoy the adventure along the way.

Go pursue your passion, and have fun as you travel from where you are to where you want to be.

Lou Mongello
Host of WDW Radio

INTRODUCTION

From Fear to Fun

I've always been an entrepreneur. Ever since I knew I wanted to do more than sell encyclopedias door-to-door (yes, I actually sold those!), I've worked for myself. I knew that I could never even come close to being satisfied if I was working for someone else.

Once I made that decision, I knew things were going to work out. There were most definitely times when I had reason to wonder if I'd made the right decision. But shortly after I had those doubts, something would happen to show me that I was on the right track.

I was fortunate enough to be on the roller-coaster ride that was the first dot-com boom. In the late nineties, venture capitalists were throwing millions of dollars at anything with ".com" at the end of it. You could have registered MonkeyUnderwear.com and raised capital in those days!

I didn't need to go the venture capital route since my content sites were making bank through affiliate promotions. I like to refer to affiliate marketing as SOPS, or Selling Other People's Stuff. Basically the way it works is that you link to a product and the merchant is able to track all sales back to where the click originated. I was riding high on some serious affiliate income. And then it happened.

The unsustainable business models came crashing down as the dot-com bubble burst. The NASDAQ plummeted from 5,000 to 2,000, leaving many investors holding a big bag of nothing.

As you might expect, my revenue stream dried up over the course of that year, and I found myself wondering what to do next.

The thing was, I knew Internet commerce wasn't a fad. While others were questioning if online business would ever survive, I had a gut feeling. I knew that it would, and I knew that I knew it would. I even knew that I knew that I knew that—well, you get the idea. I had faith that all would be well. The only question was how long it would take for it to come back.

Needless to say, it did come back—with a vengeance. In fact, the second boom was bigger than the first and continues to this day. More about how that happened later in the book.

There have been moments since then that have been no less stressful. I've had to downsize and lay people off. I've wondered whether a product my team had created would sell, and yes, I've had failures. It happens in every business.

But there's one thing I've found throughout my business

life that has always held true. When I've had the most fun, I've had the most success. And it was when I found the activity that I enjoyed the most—talking to other entrepreneurs, creating new products and services, and helping other people succeed—that I found the greatest meaning. It's also those moments that create the highest RoE for me, or Return on Experience.

It's true that life is not a destination but a journey. It is the day-by-day moments we experience, and the people we experience those moments with, that make us truly alive. When Professor John Keating (played by the brilliant late Robin Williams) stood before his students in the film *Dead Poet's Society* and admonished them to *carpe diem*, he nailed it.

Influenced by the message of the film, I have attempted to seize the day and surrender to the current moment or season of life to take me where it may. In fact, I see the world as a place resplendent with sandboxes of possibility. And I'm just a guy with a pail and a shovel, looking for sandboxes to play in. Sometimes I'll build something that gets swept away by the tide, and sometimes I'll build a castle that stands against the elements. It's the reward of this childlike wonder and genuine curiosity that motivates and inspires me to stay on this unpredictable path.

It's served me quite well in business.

I love computer games, so when my webmaster pointed out the pet project of a University of California grad student in 1996, I was all ears. Eron Jokipii had developed the foundations of one of the web's first multiplayer game rooms. Populated by a handful of his friends, the Java-based code allowed others to gather with friends and play a variety of card and table games such as hearts, chess, checkers, and backgammon.

It didn't take much persuasion to invite Eron to partner with me. He would continue to code and build the site while I would market it to the public and develop an audience. As he and I executed our roles, the site took off and caught the attention of the web's biggest search engine at the time, Yahoo!

The site was eventually acquired by Yahoo! and became the starting point for Yahoo! Games. With Eron as my partner, I was able to secure my first seven-figure deal on the web. The money was the payoff for having fun creating and marketing something that we believed in.

The "pail and shovel" mind-set has also served me well in expanding my horizons.

In a future chapter I'll share a bit about a semi-sabbatical I embarked upon during a difficult season in my business and personal life. Toward the end of this time when I was semi-retired, I decided to shake my paradigm and do something entirely unique for an entrepreneur such as myself. I chose to get a job!

I'm talking about a minimum-wage, one- or two-shifts-per-week job. Not for the money (obviously), but for the experience. I ended up securing a position at the only place a *New York Times* bestselling author could: a retail bookstore!

The experience was quite valuable and a great deal of fun. Spending time behind the cash register of a big-box store provided a much-needed shift as I prepared to reemerge as an author and speaker. I'll share more later about how my experience and the story I took away from it became something that would inspire others. That's what happens when you step outside your comfort zone without expectations. New discoveries unfold with each new experience, and our lives truly become our classroom.

Finally, looking at life through the lens of fun has impacted me the most where it matters most: in my relationships.

When I am speaking to groups I have a great time. That's one reason people connect with me. We are drawn to people who seem to be having a good time. It's magnetic. Fun isn't a game and it isn't just for children. It's a way of life!

That should always be our goal. Not to earn more money. Not to buy a bigger TV. Not to move the parking space a little closer to the office entrance. But to be happy. To have fun. To find the things in life that give us meaning. And to pay it forward so in sharing your fun, others can discover their own.

In the first chapter, I'm going to look at some of the things that hold us back not only from finding that meaning, but from even looking for it. Those forces are powerful and take hold over many years. They have to be recognized before they're overcome, so I'll explain the change of thinking necessary to overcome them.

In the section that follows, I'll talk about the solution. I'll discuss what it means to have fun, how to understand your place in the world, how to find the right way to work, and how to live an authentic life. I've also isolated a few case studies (I call them Fun Studies) that I believe exemplify the spirit of fun in the lives of others in business. You'll find them scattered throughout the book.

You may be suffering from burnout. You may be asking yourself tough introspective questions about what you are doing and why you are doing it. Or you may just be wanting a bit more freedom and fun in your lifestyle.

Relax. You've come to the right place. Come on this journey with me and so many others who have discovered the often ignored and understated secret to greater fulfillment in business and life. It's the forgotten formula called fun! Let's do this thing.

$\rightarrow$ 1 $\leftarrow$

HOW DID WE GET HERE?

We all come to a point in our lives when we look back and think, *How did I get here?*

For Kenyon Salo, that question is particularly difficult to answer. A motivational speaker, he's also an adventure athlete who has made more than five thousand sky dives and four hundred base jumps. He's one of the six members of the Denver Broncos Thunderstorm Skydive Team. Each week that the Broncos play at home, he takes a plane into the skies over Denver, jumps out, then flies at sixty miles per hour into Sports Authority Field to land on his toes on the ten-yard line. He's watched the Broncos play many games, but he's never once had to buy a ticket or stand in line at the turnstile.

For most of us, standing at the open door of an airplane a few thousand feet above a stadium and preparing to jump would prompt a very different question. We'd be less likely to ask *how* we got there than, *What the heck am I doing here?!*

For Kenyon Salo, the answer to that question would be simple. It would be, "I'm doing exactly what I've always wanted to do."

Few people are fortunate enough to say that about their work. Few of us knew when we were kids exactly what we wanted from life. Some kids know. They're the ones who study the right topics, get the right grades, and hey presto, twenty years later they're holding a wrench and floating around the space station fixing air leaks. Or jumping out of planes above stadiums.

But that's not usually how life goes. We might start by dreaming of becoming a secret agent or a test pilot or a fashion designer or a rock star. But once we accept that those exciting things are pretty unlikely, we struggle to find something to replace them with, so that by the time we leave school and even by the time we leave college, many of us are still pretty directionless. In one study of 1,025 teens aged fourteen to eighteen, 15 percent said they didn't know what they wanted to do in life. Fourteen percent indicated that they wanted to do "something in the arts," and 9 percent were hoping to work in sports. Just 12 percent said they wanted to be entrepreneurs.[1]

And yet, we all get somewhere!

It might not be what we intended. It might not be anything we would have once considered. But by the time we hit middle age, we've traveled half our journey. We've done it without a map, and we are where we are, intended or not.

So what propelled us? How did we find our way? And what did we learn about ourselves during that journey?

HARD WORK FUELS THE TRIP

We are given a mind-set by our parents, our peers, our teachers, and society. It's a Western, American work ethic that says if you want to succeed in life, you have to work hard.

We've had that drummed into us so much that it's gospel: work hard to achieve what you want. Even the Bible talks about the value of hard work: "The one who is unwilling to work shall not eat" (2 Thess. 3:10).

We embrace without question the idea that working hard is good in itself, because we see our parents go to work. We go to school where we study hard so that we can become something. We remind kids of the result of hard work each time we ask them what they want to be when they grow up or what major they want to study in college. We reward the achievements that come from hard work.

Everything is based on a notion of performance, and that performance seeps into our attitude about how people see us: if we work hard, we achieve; and if we achieve, we are accepted.

This mind-set was ingrained in me as it was most likely ingrained in you. We automatically accept it as truth. This is what we are supposed to do. Throughout our childhood, we're graded and rated.

None of this is done with malicious intent. One of the benefits of this work ethic is that we are encouraged to try—and try again when we don't win. I mostly taught myself how to play the piano, and I entirely taught myself how to play the drums. It took time and practice. To learn how to play the drums I had to sit down, put the headphones on with the music I wanted to play, and keep at it until I could hold the rhythm. It never just happened (as I'm sure my neighbors will be happy to tell you). Sure, some people are naturally gifted in some things, but that only means they have to work hard to reach excellence while the rest of us have to work even harder to reach competence. For all of those hours spent beating away at the drum kit, I'm never going to supply backing rhythms for Imagine Dragons.

There are some things that no amount of hard work can fix. In high school I hated chemistry. I don't know if it was the teacher or the smell of the lab, but it just never clicked with me. To this day I can't balance a chemistry equation and I wouldn't want to try. I got a D in chemistry, which was a big thing at the time. It was the only D I ever got. Today, it makes no difference to me at all. I don't need to know the molecular structure of sodium chloride when I'm putting together a talk for a Fortune 500 company.

Everyone needs to have certain basic skills, such as reading, writing, and arithmetic, but for the rest, we put everybody into the same mixer and say everybody needs to have this blend of science, history, social studies, home economics, and so forth. We expect everybody to learn on the same level and share a passion to learn things that they just have no interest in.

In my family we homeschooled our kids when they were young so that we could best serve their *individual* needs. Some teachers see individual children and work with them on their specific talents, but in general, education is a system, and when you combine that system with the Protestant work ethic, you get confusion.

We put a great deal of effort into some topics and get nowhere (that was my experience with chemistry). We put the same effort into other topics and get somewhere. It might not be very far, but it's a start and the journey is fun (that was my experience with drumming). But there are some topics that feel effortless because we enjoy them so much. That's when we go the farthest.

The enjoyment you felt by working hard on these kinds of subjects is the fuel that's driven you to where you are now. You discovered, through trial and error probably, the activities that gave you the greatest rewards for the least amount of work. Not necessarily the least amount of *effort*, because you still put in the hours, but it didn't feel like work because it was so much fun. You enjoyed it. That's what we should be encouraging people to do: be willing to play.

The *Oxford English Dictionary* defines *play* as "to engage in activity for enjoyment and recreation rather than a serious or practical purpose."[2] No practical purpose? Someone needs to remind Oxford what play is all about.

Play is how I ended up where I am. I'm in my midfifties

now, and I don't ever want to lose the ability to think, *That sounds fun. I want to try that! I want to go there. I want to meet this person. I want to have this experience.*

When people ask me what I do for a living, I still say, "I play." I don't say, "I am . . ." in the way that people say, "I'm a lawyer" or "I'm a doctor." They find an identity in the task they accomplish rather than in who they are as a human being.

What I want to do is inspire people to be human first and let the passions that come from their humanity lead them to do the things that interest them the most. That's where the magic happens. That's where movement happens without hard work. (I hope you highlighted this last bit. It's important.)

It's not as though life is a straight line. It's rare that our plans go according to blueprint. You might have planned on being a doctor and even gone through medical school only to discover that your real passion is helping people select a life insurance plan. A change in relationship status or the addition of a newborn (surprise, it's a girl!) can have the same effect. The point is, we often can't anticipate what we'll discover about ourselves or the circumstances that will dramatically affect our lives. Regardless of how the pivots and 180-degree turnarounds occur, it usually takes recognizing that we are lost in order to reorient and find our way.

GETTING LOST ALONG THE WAY

In 2015 the American Gap Association, an organization that helps students take a gap year before heading off to college, gave out some $2.8 million in scholarships and grants. Since 2010, attendance at gap year fairs has risen nearly threefold.[3] Asked why they were looking to take a gap year, 92 percent of students said they wanted to gain life experience or grow personally. Eighty-five percent said they wanted to travel and experience other cultures. Fewer than half said they were taking a gap year to explore career options. (And when it came to the most significant experiences they had during a gap year, partying was one of the least cited.)[4]

No one criticizes young people when they take that year off. In fact, nearly one gap year student in three said that their parents and peers actually encouraged them to do it. But for people in their thirties, forties, or fifties, it's not okay by society's standards to head off the road and try a different path for a while. I've had many conversations with people in which they say, "I am interested in this. I like this, but I don't know how to make anything of it."

People should find a way to make something of it, whatever "it" is. In your twenties, you're ready to take on the world. You want to take all the knowledge you think you have and change everything. In your thirties, you might start to feel a little disillusioned. This is when you start to think that this isn't going exactly as you thought it would. In your forties you think, *I don't know what the heck I'm doing,* and in your fifties you think, *Not only don't I know what the heck I'm doing, but I don't care because I'm just going to do it anyhow.* This makes me wonder what I'll be thinking in my sixties and seventies!

We all experience being lost in some phases of our lives.

Whether it's personal, business, or spiritual, there are moments when you have to stop and look for a landmark. Those are the moments that cause us to seek and learn and grow. If you think you know where you are all the time, it's because you're too busy looking down at the path instead of looking around you. Life is dynamic. The scenery changes. Just when you think you've got it figured out, you meet a big obstacle. Or you come to the end of the road and you have to turn around and go back the way you came.

Sometimes it's sudden. Marriages that look good suddenly break. Buyers you've trusted tell you they can't pay their bills, killing your cash flow and bringing down the business. Things happen. Sometimes you could have seen the signs if you had paid attention. Other times there's nothing you can do but pick yourself up and change direction.

In time you come to learn that something is always coming. No road ever runs straight. So we have to be able to adapt and shift and recognize that what is right now is not necessarily forever, whether that's a business model or even a relationship. Even if everything continues, it will change, and you have to be willing to adapt to those changes.

Fear is what keeps people from seeing those changes. We don't want to look at them, and we don't want to think about the challenge of adapting. It's understandable. Change can be tough, even when it takes you where you want to go. Kenyon Salo now has one of the best jobs in the world, but what brought him to that job was some effort, of course. He became a pro snowboarder first by snowboarding all day while working nights for a property maintenance company in Colorado.

CHANGE CAN BE TOUGH, EVEN WHEN IT TAKES YOU WHERE YOU WANT TO GO.

He became a professional parachutist by doing what he loved in his spare time.

"There are times when you have to buckle down and do what needs to be done," he says. Even if that means doing two or even three things at the same time. "During the day you're doing your nine-to-five job, then you come home and you're doing that other thing. And you keep focusing on that until twelve or two in the morning, or whatever it is."

"Eventually," he says, "you're able to make the leap from one to the other."

TRAVELING AS A GROUP

Kenyon Salo isn't just unusual for being able to jump out of planes for a living. He's also unusual in that he was able to strike out on his own path. Plenty of people probably told him that he was crazy for trying to do what he wanted to do.

Those messages have an effect. We are easily shamed. Without a strong sense of self, we tend to go with the flow of what our peer group wants to do. Our own dreams and hopes and desires get squashed. We find ourselves thinking: *Well, if they say this is stupid, it must be stupid. Or I must be stupid because I must be missing something. If I was normal I would do what they want me to do.*

Peer pressure affects us so much more than pressure from our parents or from our teachers. We often value what our peers think—the people that we meet in school or at work— more than the opinion of anybody else. We want to fit in, but fitting in isn't all it's cracked up to be. The people who are the most fulfilled are often the ones who have truly learned to not care what other people think.

It's hard to do that. I still catch myself, even at half a century old, caring about what somebody is going to think of me. But I'm aware of it, and that helps. Once we are aware of not only what we are thinking but *why* we are thinking it, we can take action and change our thinking. We can tell ourselves: *I don't have to live like that. I don't have to put up with that. Who made these rules for me, and when did I decide that I was going to abide by these rules?*

Pressure happens within families but in a subtler way. If you grew up in a family where your father was imposing and a doctor, then you might feel pressure to be a doctor or maybe a lawyer. You are going to go to school and become a professional because you are living somebody else's dream. Your own dream to run a carpentry store or become a dancer or whatever gets left behind. You lose yourself.

I've known people who fell into that trap. They became professionals and for decades built successful but unfulfilling careers that they couldn't leave because of the money they were making. They had financial commitments, a mortgage, a certain lifestyle, and they couldn't see a way out. They were told that was the choice they'd made and that they had to live with it. And that is not the case.

There's always a way out: sell the house, stop buying stuff, scale down, quit your job, and do something else. You always have to be responsible, of course. There are times in our lives when we have to do things we don't want to do. Kenyon Salo kept working for that property maintenance company even when he was building his snowboarding skills. You might have to work two or three jobs to make ends meet, but that doesn't mean you can't dream while you are working. It doesn't mean you can't start thinking, listening to your heart, and asking yourself questions.

Everything has its season; it's not all sunshine and rainbows. But the hardest parts of the journey don't last forever.

REGRET FOR THE PATH NOT TAKEN

Bronnie Ware is an Australian nurse who spent a number of years helping people in the last twelve weeks of their lives. As she cared for them, she asked them about their lives and how they felt as they approached the end. She put their answers together in a book called *The Top Five Regrets of the Dying*.

Some of those regrets were predictable. Men in particular wished that they had worked less and spent more time with their families. Everyone wished that they had invested more in friendships and stayed in touch with old friends. People wished that they had expressed their feelings more; some even felt that their illnesses were a result of the resentment and bitterness that they had allowed to build.

But two regrets stood out. People wished that they had allowed themselves to be happier, and they wished that they'd had the courage to live a life that was true to themselves and not the life that others expected of them.[5]

It might be inevitable. When we reach the end of the

journey, we will always be able to look back and see the trail-heads we didn't take, the paths we didn't choose. Maybe at the end there should even be a curiosity about what lay down those paths. But ultimately are you going to look back at your life and say, "I'm glad I succumbed to peer pressure and didn't follow my passion or my dreams or my desires"? Or are you going to say, "I'm glad I did what I wanted to do regardless of what anybody else thought"? You might wish that you had stayed in closer contact with your friends as your life progressed, but you won't remember the people who put pressure on you to walk with them instead of forging your own path.

Being told by society what we can and can't do is never going to lead us to fulfillment. It will never take us where we want to go. When we look at history, we recognize people who did extraordinary things, the people who went out on a limb to do something that nobody else would attempt or nobody else succeeded at doing. People might have called them crazy. They might have laughed at them. But when those brave ones reached their destination, they could look back and know that they were always in control of the route—even if that route was plummeting at sixty miles per hour straight down and into a football stadium.

In the next chapter, we'll look at how to take that control.

⇒ 2 ⇐

A NEW APPROACH TO LIFE

When I was twelve years old, my parents divorced. That's not unusual. Today, nearly half of all marriages break up, and we have to hope that each partner overcomes the initial pain and goes on to find a path that's more fulfilling.

It's hard to see that at the time though. The process of divorce is always painful and difficult, and it's impossible to know until it's over what lies at the end. Whenever change happens, whether we're children or grown-up, we feel a real sense of powerlessness. Change is overwhelming. We can't imagine what our lives will be like next. It's terrifying.

As a result, fear of change is present in every aspect of our lives. We dread the pain that could wait for us over the horizon, and we do everything we can to avoid that potential discomfort. That is why we quit our addictions and our vices only when the consequences of indulging them hurt us or others more than the pain of quitting them.

It's only when you have a heart attack and the doctor says you really need to quit scarfing hamburgers, or your spouse is giving you the stink eye because you are working all hours of the day and are never with the kids, that you look again at where you are and think, *Maybe I need to change this*.

We reach a point where we're willing to make some changes to avoid facing something more painful in the future. More often, though, we don't have a choice. The pain we fear arrives, and we have to make the changes that we were afraid to make and face all those uncertainties that stopped us from taking action before. The hammer falls. The job goes. The spouse leaves and takes the kids.

It's so much easier to pretend that we live in a world of certainty. It's much more comforting to believe that we can bank on getting up in the morning and going to work the next day. It's not true. Only in a make-believe world is job security a thing. Something can happen, and it will. It always does.

JOEL'S LAW: WHAT CAN CHANGE WILL CHANGE. AND CHANGE IS GOOD.

I don't know if I fully believe in Murphy's Law—that anything that can go wrong will go wrong—but I will offer Joel's Law: anything that can change *will* change.

Change came suddenly to E. Brian Rose. A former professional poker player, Brian had built a business introducing the world to the professional poker circuit. He traveled the world, interviewed celebrities and professional poker players, and uploaded the films to YouTube. Each episode had around eight million views and was supported by online poker sites. He even moved to Las Vegas to be closer to the action.

Then the US Senate passed the SAFE Port Act, a bill to secure the nation's ports, and somehow, along with that bill, the Senate slipped in the Unlawful Internet Gambling Enforcement Act. Online poker sites in the US were banned.

"My phone started ringing first thing in the morning," Brian recalls. "It was all my sponsors telling me that they were pulling their US advertising. I was essentially out of a job."

The business that Brian had built over the years, had invested in and enjoyed creating, was wiped out by the stroke of a government pen.

Change comes, and it's not always for the worse. (Brian went on to even bigger and better things.) But change keeps us from controlling our lives. So we let ourselves believe that we have certainty until we realize, often not until our thirties, that we don't.

Control is an illusion. We get to micromanage certain small parts of our lives, and that makes us feel in control, but the reality is that even the self-employed control very few parts of their lives, and employees control even less.

Real freedom comes with the paradigm shift of understanding that, ultimately, we really don't have much control. When we recognize that so much is out of our hands, then

REAL FREEDOM COMES WITH THE PARADIGM SHIFT OF UNDERSTANDING THAT, ULTIMATELY, WE REALLY DON'T HAVE MUCH CONTROL.

taking risks is a safer play because it gives us many more options. We get to see our lives not as a narrow path with dangers on either side but as a corridor with doors and windows that lead to new opportunities.

Some of those doors and windows are wide open. Some are open just a crack and just waiting for someone to give them a push. And some are closed, sometimes firmly. We get to choose which door we try to open, and it's not always the most obvious.

We are often told that if we really want something, we should just bang on that door until it busts open. When we meet an obstacle, we should keep pushing at it until it gives way. But for most of us, there's more than one route to where we want to go. Focusing on that one door because we believe we know what's on the other side misses all the other opportunities that might require less effort and be at least as fulfilling. If we can put aside the fear of the change that lies behind those other doors, we'll have so many more chances to take and so much less effort to make the most of them.

The paradigm so many people are stuck in is that they do their job from nine to five. Or if they're self-employed, they buy into this mentality that they have to hustle and grind and work late and stay at the desk on weekends because if they don't, some other guy is going to come along and take their milk money. That is not living. That is being a servant to the J-O-B, which many people refer to as "Just Over Broke."

There's a meme that goes around the internet pretty regularly. It pictures the ultimate worker bee, Dwight Schrute from *The Office*. The top of the meme says, "Life is short," and underneath Schrute's glance it says, "False. It's the longest thing we do." As profound as that truth is, our time on this planet *is* brief. So we need to find a balance that lets us enjoy the experience now, with the people we are with and the circumstances we are in, rather than just toiling away. We need to be curious enough about those other doors and ready for the change that lies behind them to walk away from the sealed door we think we know. We need to try an easier one and a more enjoyable path however scary that change might look. That's when the magic happens.

THERE ARE EXPERIENCES AND GOALS BEHIND THOSE DOORS

Some people are goal oriented. It could be a personality type or it could be learned, but some subscribe to goal-setting as a way of life. They need to know their short-term goals, their medium-term goals, and their long-term goals. It gives them a sense of direction and security.

After Chris Guillebeau finished college, he headed off to West Africa and spent four years volunteering on a hospital ship. That experience only gave him a taste for more travel; the more countries he saw, the more interested he became in the exploration process and discovering new places. "After I'd done that without a goal for thirty to fifty countries, I started to think about what if I made this into something of a quest," he recalls. "What if I made this bigger?"

Chris set himself a target. He planned to visit all 193 countries in the world.

For Chris, the plan worked. He traveled the world. About halfway through, he started a blog describing his trips. He soon found that he was better at writing about the mechanics of travel than describing places, and he won an audience for his travel hacks. By the time he returned from the last country, he had a book contract and opportunities to make money as a professional speaker.

Goal setting is fine if it works for you. But if somebody told me I needed to set goals, I'd question it. I'd want to know why.

All I know is that over the next year I'm going to turn a lot of doorknobs, walk through a lot of entryways, and have experiences and opportunities that I didn't expect. I'm going to meet people. I'm going to do things that will change what I thought would happen. I'll be surprised.

I've learned to trust the process. There's a saying that man plans and God laughs. But it's not just our plans that he laughs at. It's also our assumptions. We often find that everything we believed about a person was untrue, sometimes for better and sometimes for worse. We assume that a job we're doing will take us to a particular destination, only to find that it isn't what we want at all.

Life unfolds in ways that we just don't expect. The only thing that we *can* expect is the unexpected. We have to go with the flow and be open to those opportunities as life is happening around us.

That attitude demands patience. Success rarely happens

overnight, and it's often built on a pile of failures. My first book taught people the techniques that I'd used to achieve extraordinary passive income with Google's AdSense system, but those revenues didn't come to me immediately—and they didn't come immediately to the many people who read and used that book either. Instead, the most important lesson in that book was to keep testing: try different styles, different keywords, different placements, different ad sizes. Keep changing the ads, and with each change, income grows. It takes time, but you get there, and the results are surprising. People often found that it was the topics they didn't expect that produced the highest revenues, and that discovery changed the direction of their website and gave them a whole new interest. Their goal might have been to reach a particular revenue level by a particular date, but to reach that goal they had to be patient, and they had to be prepared to change their plans.

It takes courage to make that change. Brenton Weyi is a speaker, entrepreneur, and writer who was invited by a nonprofit agency to work with a global accelerator in Brazil. After his stay ended, the agency offered Brenton a full-time job. It was an impressive opportunity, a chance to make a difference, and whenever Brenton would talk about his work with others, listeners were always impressed. "That must be the greatest job ever," they'd say, and they'd mean it.

But for Brenton, there was always a sense of friction. "I just had this niggling feeling in the back of my mind that made me feel that I wasn't doing the right thing," he recalls. "I got high on the emotion but not on the actual purpose."

Brenton was getting some of the benefits that he expected

the job to deliver and which to many people are sufficient—the salary, of course, but also the praise and the accolades. But it wasn't *fun*.

It wasn't long before a project the agency was working on hit a rough patch, and the positivity that had held Brenton at the agency began to disappear. Those changing circumstances were exactly what he needed to make a change and find a new direction, even if it took him away from a road that looked, from the outside, very attractive. It took him on a path that was more meaningful for him.

GRATITUDE IS THE POWER TO CHANGE DIRECTION

Knowing that change is inevitable enables us to express gratitude for what we have right now. And we all have things for which we should feel grateful: for being alive, for being healthy, for having the strength to push through any physical ailments, for reading this book (!), for the people in your life, and for communities where you can find people to add to your life.

If we come from a place of gratitude, we have joy. We don't feel that something needs to happen in order to feel that *this* is our day. We can live in a permanent state of "I'm good." We don't need something else to be happy but can rest in a place of contentment where we are.

That gratitude and that joy come when you focus on living rather than on grinding every day—and with it comes trust. You learn to trust yourself. You learn to know yourself.

You learn to listen to your heart and to squash the voices that you have absorbed from parents and teachers and peers and society. Those are the voices that, when you take them as truth, suck the fun out of life.

Part of trusting the process is trusting those things that light you up, those things that make you think: *I really want to do that.* When you have that trust, you can just do it. You don't have to wait. You don't have to hope that tomorrow brings you a chance to make the change you want. You have the power to do it—and to do it now.

You can make your first move today because you don't know what tomorrow will bring. You can begin the process immediately. You can do a little right now and come back in a few days and do some more. You can trust that you'll get out there and you'll make it right.

You find then that your attitude is completely different from somebody who has been hired to complete a similar task—someone whose head is in their work but whose heart isn't. When your heart is there, your chances of being successful and having an impact increase exponentially.

YOU DON'T HAVE TO DO WHAT YOU DON'T WANT TO DO

Nearly everything in life falls on one of two sides of a spectrum. Something is either life giving or it is life taking. It either feeds your soul or it sucks from your soul. You can feel that sucking happen. It's as though your energy and life force are being depleted at a rapidly accelerating pace. If there is a task in your life that is vacuuming away portions of your soul, then you have to ask whether you are the right person for the task. You have to ask yourself why you chose to do it, whether you made that decision because you felt you should or because you were forced through guilt or codependency to take on a task that you really didn't want in the first place.

When you work with resentment, *that* sucks your soul. But if you work with joy, then it is life giving both for you and for the person you are doing it for. And the job is more likely to be done exceedingly well.

How many times has someone told you what you should do about something? You know what I'm talking about. Maybe you are even guilty of doing it to someone else. I know I am.

But I propose that you don't ever let anyone "should" on you. Don't let anyone tell you that you "should" write this or go there or be with this person or get married or get divorced or move here or take this job or leave that job. When we hear that "should" as adults, what we're actually hearing is people telling us how to live our lives. They shouldn't do that. (Oh snap, did I just do it?)

The bottom line is that *you* get to decide. You're in charge. As the great American philosopher Jon Bon Jovi said in his hit song, "It's My life!" Ultimately, nobody else has to answer for your life but you. When you recognize that truth, you'll be empowered to change. You'll throw off the fear of change. You'll be prepared to walk through any of the doors that appeal to you. And you'll have a whole new attitude toward life.

THE MOMENT YOU CHOOSE TO HAVE FUN

Catch sight of Felicia Slattery as she flies down a roller coaster at Dollywood, her favorite amusement park, and you'll be seeing someone who knows how to have fun. But what you won't see—and is often difficult to see in people who have found a way to seize every day—is the moment she made that choice.

It's a moment that everyone who has turned their work into fun has encountered. They realize that however much success they might have created, however many goals they might have achieved, there's still something missing. Or they might realize that however hard they're working, they're not moving forward—and the reason they're not moving forward is that their heart isn't in it. Those moments demand a reevaluation of choices.

For Felicia Slattery, that moment came in a hospital bed. It was 2004 and she was thirty-four weeks pregnant with her second daughter. She had contracted a rare and painful pregnancy illness, and the doctors estimated that she had between four and eight hours to live.

Felicia and her child survived. But the recovery took time. As she contemplated what she would do when her health and strength returned and her maternity break ended, she understood that her life was a gift and not something she could waste. She needed to do something that would allow her to make the most of the years she had miraculously managed to retain. She wanted a career that would allow her to build a business from home while looking after what she called her two "angel babies." In 2006, two years after contracting a near-fatal illness, Felicia launched a coaching and consulting firm.

Today, Felicia can be seen on stage at business conferences. She's addressed firms as large as Kohler and Kraft, helping their employees to understand how to network and present ideas. She's leading the life that she feels she was meant to lead. The only experience that could be more enjoyable is a day with her husband and two children, riding the Mystery Mine at Dollywood.

⇒ 3 ⇐

WHAT DOES FUN EVEN MEAN?

Alex Pang is a technology forecaster and consultant in Silicon Valley. After fifteen years of long projects, multitasking, and plenty of travel, he was feeling the effects of burnout. At first he did what many people do when they feel they're falling behind. He tried to work longer hours. If he was feeling the pressure, he thought, then more work would relieve the pressure. When that failed, he tried the opposite approach and took a sabbatical at Microsoft Research in Cambridge. "I found that in three months I got an enormous amount of stuff done and did an awful lot of really serious thinking, which was a great luxury, but I also had what felt like an amazingly leisurely life," he told *The Guardian* newspaper.

Without the pressure to look busy or the stress that came with consulting, he was able to achieve more—and had more fun doing it. He started to rethink the idea that more hours equal more productivity, and he came to realize that rest is not the absence of work but something necessary to work effectively.[1]

"Rest is not work's adversary," he wrote in his book *Rest: Why You Get More Done When You Work Less*. "Rest is work's partner. They complement and complete each other."[2]

Research supports that idea. Studies conducted in the 1950s found that scientists who spent twenty-five hours in the workplace each week were no more productive than those who spent just five hours at work. People who worked twenty hours a week were twice as productive as those working thirty-five hours a week, while people who put in as much as sixty hours or more were the least productive.[3]

So working long hours doesn't produce the best results. If you're focusing on the number of hours you're punching on your time card, you're in the wrong mind-set. It doesn't bring happiness, it doesn't bring results, and it's not fun.

Fun is not what we do. It's a way of life, a way of approaching everything in our life holistically—whether it's business or pleasure—following our hearts and our passions without forgetting the childlike curiosity that is still in all of us. Our bodies have maybe aged a bit (and widened a bit more), but in many ways we're still that same person that we were when we were young. The adult world can squeeze that sense of fun out of us, but when we get in touch with the joy we had as children, we bring that adventurousness into our adultness. That's why I like to say that I've got "adulting" down to a

FUN IS NOT WHAT WE DO. IT'S A WAY OF LIFE.

science. I take care of what needs to be taken care of. I'm a responsible person. But the whole "grown-up" thing? No, I'll never get that down. I'd rather be like Peter Pan, only more responsible (and yet with the ability to fly, please).

If we're doing what we love instead of just putting in the hours we think we should, we're going to be more invested in what we do because we *care* about it. And we'll be more successful as a result.

PUTTING THE FUN IN FULFILLMENT

Turn on the television, and eventually you'll see an ad with a smiling, happy person who's full of joy. He's happy because he's now got the right cheese to put on his hamburger, and it's brought fulfillment to his life. Or we'll see the look of satisfaction on the face of someone who has the right insurance agent or just enough money, or the right house in the right location with the perfect spouse, 2.4 kids (always felt sorry for that child that was just 40 percent of a person), and the fenced yard with the dog.

Anybody who's achieved anything will tell you that it feels great to have the accomplishment. But the fulfillment that comes with achievement passes. When you reach that goal, whether it's a big raise, a successful product launch, or even an Academy Award, it's a great moment and we should strive for those great moments. But those moments do not define who we are. If they did, then who would we be without those things? Do we have less value because we didn't win the award or write the song? If we don't make a giant salary, land the job we wanted, or marry a supermodel, are we less than we thought we were? Of course not. We still have the same intrinsic value, significance, and desire for unconditional love.

Achievements can be mountaintop experiences. But we don't live on the mountain. It's cold up there and it can get lonely. Inevitably, we come back down, and doing so can be depressing and depleting. Back in the valley, things can get really tough. Real life sets in again, but you still remember the view from the top.

We go up the mountain. We come down the mountain. Up. Down. Up. Down. Life, work, and all the unexpected twists and turns can be exhausting physically, emotionally, mentally, and spiritually. In fact, even without the highs and lows, striving to find some sort of balance is a challenge all its own. But is it truly possible to find balance, or is life truly lived in imbalance?

WORK-LIFE BALANCE IS A MYTH

The idea of a work-life balance is a myth. The seesaw never stays level. The moment when it's balanced and perfectly still is fragile and temporary. That position doesn't last. We'll never have permanent balance until we're no longer breathing.

The most common state isn't a work-life balance but a work-life imbalance, and we always know internally when we're off-kilter. We know when we're spending too much time working. We know when we're goofing off too much. And it's up to us to decide what adjustment we really want to make.

The move from a work-life balance to a life in which work is inseparable from fun always starts with a decision. It begins with the recognition that your life isn't bringing you fulfillment and the acceptance that something has to change. If the decision is to cut back on the hours in the office in favor of time with family or activities you find more fulfilling, where do you start?

That question isn't as hard to answer as it sounds. People who believe they need to have the job to support the house and the vacations and the big cars also believe that there's no way out. There could be a way out. They could downsize and get a smaller house. Dump some of the stuff. Eliminate some expenses. Then, perhaps, they could take another job. The options are there. If they open up their mind to the idea that they can do almost anything they want, including selling everything, then everything is open. They're not tied down anymore.

It all starts with a decision—a decision to find your fun.

FINDING YOUR FUN

Making the decision to find fun isn't difficult. But finding *your* fun can be a challenge.

David Hancock didn't like books when he was young. He resisted reading in high school. He avoided books in college. It wasn't until he was running his own property business and wanted to know how to do it easier, better, and faster that he started picking up nonfiction books. He began with *Who Moved My Cheese* and worked his way through other business books. Each morning he would read, and each afternoon he would test what he had read by applying it to his business and seeing if he made money with it.

He followed that principle when he moved from building to mortgage banking, and he found it so effective that he opened a publishing company in his spare time. He's now the owner of Morgan James, an entrepreneurial publisher that publishes 125 nonfiction books written by business leaders every year. The business hasn't just helped leaders find their audiences and entrepreneurs acquire knowledge, it's also brought David a new level of fulfillment.

"It was hard for me to get balance into my life," he says. "The more I resisted, the less fun I was having. Now balancing faith, family, food, and fun with work has made my life so much more fun."

A good place to start looking for your fun is with a list of all the things that make up your life—your work, your relationships, your goals—and asking yourself how happy you are with each of them. Really evaluate how you feel about the current state of your life.

That won't be easy because we've already seen that no one likes change. Our brains will fight to maintain the status quo. We'll make excuses, and we have to be able to identify those excuses.

You'll need to be brutally honest with yourself. You'll need to be willing to investigate your own life, make an assessment, and then think about what makes you happy. It could be playing music. It could be writing. It could be painting. It could be debating. It could be helping others. There are so many different ways that we can demonstrate our gifts in the world. Go back to what used to make you happy—whether it was last week, last year, a decade ago, or when you were a kid. Think about how you were creative or analytical. What did you do as a child that brought you a sense of joy and purpose? There are clues there. Our life leaves little bread crumbs that lead us to where we should go.

All the things we learn in the different occupations that we participate in, especially the ones that interest us, come around again. See your life experiences as a series of building blocks of lessons learned and skills acquired. Those lessons and skills become the new foundation to "level up" to the next experience that will come your way.

After a while, you'll probably find yourself wondering who you really are. Let's explore that in the next chapter.

Are we having fun yet?

⇥ 4 ⇤

WHO AM I?

After my partner and I sold our gaming site to Yahoo, I had the chance to meet with one of the company's entertainment VPs. "We're launching a kids' site," he told me. "Would you be interested in coming on our team?"

Yahooligans, Yahoo's portal for kids, turned out to be one of the most creative things that Yahoo would build, and the opportunity was awesome: a fun business idea, a good company, a great salary with Silicon Valley benefits.

It took me just one second to know how I would answer. Here's why.

I believe that every single person who has ever walked the face of the earth was made with distinct passions and innate talents. We have an aptitude that inclines us toward specific skills and abilities that we pick up as we go through our lives, and each of us has a unique personality that makes us unlike anybody else.

When we take all those things—passions, talents, skills, ability, personality—and put them all together, out comes a unique individual. It sounds trite, but there really is nobody like us. Seven billion people on Earth right now. I don't know how many there were before and I don't know how many there will be after, but among all of those billions, there never was and never will be another me. There will never be another you. That's it. It's an indisputable fact.

Nothing is made without a purpose. A hammer exists to bang in nails, a saw to cut through wood. We have forks to twirl spaghetti, earbuds to listen to our favorite tunes, and little plastic tables to stop the pizza box from squashing the pizza. Everything is here for a reason. If everything we create serves a purpose, doesn't it make sense that we were created for a purpose as well?

We all have the ability to make a difference and bring value. And because we are unique, we have a unique ability to do so. However subtle or massive that impact is, we are all designed to bring value to the world.

I would go so far as to say that if we are not using our uniqueness or passions or talents or skills or ability or personality to discover that value and present it to others, we are doing the world a disservice. If you are a gifted singer and you are not using your vocal talents, you're missing something—and others are missing something. If you are a gifted teacher and are not teaching, then there are kids who are having a worse experience than they should have. Where you have an ability and don't use it, there is a piece missing from you and from the world.

WHAT DO YOU WANT TO DO?

A few people are very fortunate. They're talented in multiple areas. They can sing and dunk and code and make a perfect BLT sandwich, and they're probably really, really good-looking too. But not everyone is me. (Kidding. Seriously, the only thing worse than my cooking is my basketball skills.) Those people will have to figure out what they *want* to do the most. The rest of us have to figure out what we *can* do best, but in the end, the question is the same.

Just because you *can* do something doesn't mean you *should* do it. You will know that you *should* do it if you *want* to do it. If somebody is stopping you, if societal pressure or your own fears are "shoulding" on you, then you have to silence those voices and ask what *you* want to do.

I've been in tech as a businessman since 1995. I've done a variety of things. I started by launching a website, then moved into licensing content, affiliate marketing, internet marketing, product creation, and buying and selling websites. I've done podcasting and video creation and live video and public speaking and writing books. Those projects cover multiple areas, and each was what I wanted to do at the time. Each project brought a value. Each project gave me experience and an education. Everything I have done has taught me something.

FINDING YOUR VALUE

The result of that experimentation is magic. Fear falls. Ideas rise. Opportunities open. When you follow your passion, magic can happen. Things don't always go according to plan, but as long as you are pursuing that passion and moving forward, opportunities open that you don't even know exist.

A word of caution is in order here. Some people have a passion for something but aren't very good at it. We've all known (or been) people like that: kids who dream of playing in the NBA even though they can't dribble and will barely see over the steering wheel; friends who dream of being pop superstars but actually have voices like laryngitic frogs.

There is a saying that goes, "If you believe it, you can achieve it." I hate to burst anyone's belief bubble, but it's not true, and we know it's not true. I can *believe* that I will be an NBA star, but it's never going to happen no matter how much I want it and no matter how hard I try. I just don't have that talent—or that height. It's certainly true that if you really want something, you have to work at it. You don't become an Olympic speed skater by not putting on your skates and falling over every day. But when we tell people that all they have to do to have what they want is to want it, we're not doing them any favors.

Of course, we want to teach children to go for their dreams,

WHEN YOU FOLLOW YOUR PASSION, MAGIC CAN HAPPEN.

and when they don't yet know where their talents lie, they should dream freely. But as adults we have to look at what our skills and abilities really are.

I have always loved music and remember listening to AM radio in Chicago when I was growing up. But after dabbling with a few instruments, I realized that I would never be a real musician. I am just not good enough. That's not where my talents lie. So I became a DJ instead. After all, if you can't play your own music, why not play someone else's?

If your heart and your talent are in different places, the solution is to keep practicing, keep improving. You might never make a career of that passion, but you will have fun. Your life will be enriched by the process and the practice of your passion, even though you might never be very good at it. My piano playing is never going to get me invited to Carnegie Hall (or even a dormitory hall), but it gives me great pleasure. It's fun!

TWO WAYS TO TREAT YOUR TALENT

A couple of things are going on here. Some people have a passion for things they are good at but which they don't pursue. They might not want to pursue them or they might not feel that they're in a position to pursue them, so they keep their gifts to themselves and don't tell anyone about them. Instead, they'll pursue something else they find fun. And if they aren't in a position to do so, they'll change their position so they can. They'll move toward their talent.

Some people, though, have a passion and lack the aptitude, but they can bring something else. They love the idea of being an artist, for example, but they just don't have the hand-eye coordination that lets them turn the picture in their head into a painting on the canvas. They still need to find a way to bring drawing into their lives—and if they do that, they might well find that even though they're not the most talented person in the world, their uniqueness produces something new and special.

Scott Adams's cartoons, for example, are not highly sophisticated and technically advanced drawings. *Dilbert* is a very simple drawing, as are many of the Sunday comics. Far more cartoons are drawn with the simplicity of *Peanuts* than are sketched as elaborately as *Doonesbury*. But the power of these comics is in their wit and their ability to evoke emotion and thought.

For his book *Tools of Titans*, Tim Ferriss interviewed Ed Catmull, who's now the president of Pixar and Walt Disney Animation Studios. Catmull noted that what distinguished Pixar wasn't just its great animation and awesome storytelling. It was those things combined with amazing business sense. The combination of talents made the success.[1] Few of us are able to combine three outstanding talents in that way (and Pixar has fallen a little since the merger with Walt Disney), but combining an A- talent with a B+ skill can produce something unique and outstanding, that wins an A+ in its own small field.

We tend to compare ourselves to others, and we see our flaws. But we struggle to see the unique advantage we can bring to the talent we have. There is no shortage of doctors who can talk about health topics, but only Dr. Oz had the personality and the straight talk that could make him a star on *Oprah*.

Whenever people think that they have nothing new to say, they may be missing the true value they are able to bring. It could be that no one else is saying it. They're worried they will be laughed at or mocked or just be plain wrong. But the irony is this: that one thing that makes them different is usually their superpower. It's what makes them unique. In other words, if conventional wisdom is telling you "no one does it like that," then "that" (whatever it might be) could be your ticket to success.

Finding that uniqueness isn't simple. It's not easy to know who you are. My first clue came at that meeting at Yahoo. In less than a minute, I had turned down the job offer. Part of the reason was I had just moved my family from Texas to Oklahoma, and I didn't want to move again to California. But more importantly, I realized that I didn't want to work for anybody. I didn't want to limit my income or lose my freedom or give up on a process I had already started. I felt like that just wasn't me. Working for someone else wasn't going to make the best use of my talents.

But I knew if that decision was going to pay off, I would need to work hard—or work smart. That's the topic of the next chapter. And here's a hint: I found the way that was the most fun!

THE MANY FORMS OF FUN

It's easy to mistake success for fun. Success is satisfying. It's enjoyable. It's rewarding. Reaching a goal delivers an immediate sense of achievement. You've set a target for yourself, made a plan, and put in the effort necessary to make it happen. You've proved that you can push yourself where you want to go.

But sometimes where you think you want to go isn't the same as where you *really* want to go. And you can't know where you *really* want to go until you've seen the view from somewhere else.

That's something I experienced. Between 2008 and 2011, I built a medium-sized business. We rented a building. The offices held thirty-eight people, and if you ask me now what each person did, I might struggle to remember.

Looking back, I can see it was never something that suited me. It was pretty clear that the pressure of meeting payroll, managing the concerns of more than three dozen employees, and trying to steer a company just wasn't something I enjoyed. I might have looked successful. I might have met the standard of success that so many others set for themselves. But I wasn't having fun.

I'm not the only one who has had that experience.

Bryan Kramer is a renowned social business strategist who has spoken on the much-respected TED stage. His book *There Is No B2B or B2C: It's Human to Human #H2H* gave a valuable new perspective on social marketing. At its peak, his agency employed twenty people and was serving some of the biggest companies in the world.

But whatever fun Bryan had enjoyed as he built his business eventually faded away. The sacrifices he'd made to grow the company robbed him of the sense of satisfaction he had assumed would always be there.

"You end up giving away too many pieces so that you're no longer having fun," he recalls. "I think that happens more times than not with people who are really trying hard in business. It happened to me."

Bryan has always been a foodie and he loves to travel, so even though the company was facing major challenges, he put some distance between himself and his business. He and his wife took a trip to Europe and spent time cruising the rivers of Germany, visiting castles, and trying the local cuisine. When he came back, he wound down the company and started over as a husband-and-wife consultancy.

"We are having a much better time," he says. "The stress is less. We're feeding two, not twenty. The conversations are better, and we're taking work we love."

Fun means different things to different people. If one form of success doesn't bring you a sense of joy, it might well be time to try a different form. It might be smaller, but it could suit you better.

⇒ 5 ⇐

WORKING HARD VERSUS
WORKING SMART

My experience with Yahoo taught me a valuable lesson. It showed me how working smart was superior to working hard.

Again, this was twenty years ago. I had been dabbling with HTML but quickly discovered that I'm not a programmer. I just don't understand it, and I'm fine with that. Other people do and can crank out functional code in minutes.

My website had just a few simple web-based games. In those days you would click on something and a new page would load. Interactive, huh? But as I mentioned earlier, when my webmaster discovered the site that provided a foundation for a multiplayer game room coded in Java, I was immediately intrigued. And I could have tried to compete with it. I could have tried to learn how to code (no, thank you) or hired a coder if I'd had the money (I didn't then). Instead, I did something much easier. I reached out to the guy who had created it and suggested that we partner up. I'd bring the traffic and the marketing from my website, and he'd keep coding. As a joint venture opportunity, I wouldn't have to learn to program properly and I wouldn't have to pay him. He wouldn't have to figure out the marketing. We'd work together. It all worked out beautifully.

This all came about from recognizing an opportunity and knowing what I could bring. It took some work from both of us. But we didn't sweat it. We weren't burning the midnight oil. We each had a role, and we were doing something we both enjoyed.

We worked smart, not hard—not even for seven figures.

WORK HARD, MY SON, AND YOU'LL GO FAR

We are taught when we are young that if you work hard you can accomplish anything. This sense of rugged individualism is part of what has made America great. But it's come to mean that success is directly related not to what we do but to how long we spend doing it. Work sixteen hours a day, and you're twice as likely to succeed as someone who works eight hours a day.

We've already seen that that's not always true. The French have a saying: "If working hard made you rich, donkeys would be covered in gold."

Working smart recognizes that sometimes a small amount of effort in just the right place can have the biggest effect. Malcolm Gladwell has talked about the tipping point, the moment when a small nudge can have big results. If we can find, or create, those opportunities that are on the verge of tipping, we'll be able to produce important effects with just the lightest of touches. That is when the miracles happen.

It's the difference between being busy for the sake of busyness and making efforts that make a difference. Being active isn't enough. It's the activity itself that matters.

FIND THE HIGHEST LEVERAGE ACTIVITIES FOR YOUR GOALS AND YOU'LL GO FARTHER, FASTER

Julius Dein is a British social media star. He set himself the goal of building a huge audience online and establishing his personal brand. He built a Facebook page, uploaded videos of his magic tricks, and forged content-sharing agreements with other pages.

When he saw that his magic tricks could only take him part of the way, he cleverly moved on to pranks, which performed better. As he built momentum, he expanded his vision. He reached out to pages with larger audiences, which helped him grow faster. He made video after video, uploading as many as four a week. He'd film himself falling asleep on passengers on the London Underground. He'd run up to strangers and declare that he was their long-lost son. He'd attach a rubber snake to people's bags and watch them run off in panic.

And then he uploaded a video entitled "How to give your girlfriend the best Valentine's Day." He filmed himself waking his girlfriend with a bowl of chicken hearts, pouring ice water over her head as she read a magazine, and pushing her into a river as they took a romantic walk. In the end, he presented her with a ring in a box . . . an onion ring in a cardboard box.

The video went gangbusters. It was viewed 86 million times. Julius picked up sixty thousand likes at a rate of three hundred every ten seconds. His Facebook page raced to half a million followers. "People around the world were messaging my Facebook page so often my phone was constantly vibrating," he says. "It was incredible."

He figured out what worked and cut back on his videos. Instead of uploading several times a week and winning a few thousand views for each video, he now posts one video every three weeks but expects that video to reach an audience of millions. Brands as large as Doritos have noticed and hired him for their own videos.

"If you're going to be successful in anything, you have to treat it like a business," says Julius, before adding that what he does is a lifestyle, not a job.

Julius found the smart way to work. He identified the highest leverage activities for his goals: the point where, if you apply the right pressure with the right tool, things really start to move.

That's not always straightforward. It starts with a look at where you excel, at the best role you can take in the project. You need to recognize where your strengths are combined with what you really *enjoy* doing.

We all like to think of ourselves as superheroes. We like to believe that we can do everything: be the chief cook, the waiter, and the bottle washer. But while a chef *can* wash bottles, it's not the best use of his or her time. We're not meant to do everything. We're made to supplement and complement each other's gifts.

That is working smarter, not harder. It's using partnerships, finding people who can bring something to the table, collaborating and making deals. It's a common mistake for people to take too much on themselves, either because they think they can do everything or because they don't have the budget to outsource. But even when you're short on funds, there are often ways to share the load so that you're doing what you want to do, your partner is doing what they want to do, and you're both getting where you want to go faster.

I've already talked about how I don't like to beat down doors when there are so many other doors to explore. Another way of looking at this concept is the snowball and the mountain.

It takes a long time to create a massive snowball. And if you are creating a start-up on your own, it's like starting with a handful of snow and rolling it slowly up a mountain. The snowball gets larger as you push uphill, but it takes a long time and a great deal of effort. Once that snowball gets to the top of the mountain and reaches its tipping point, it doesn't

YOU NEED TO RECOGNIZE WHERE YOUR STRENGTHS ARE COMBINED WITH WHAT YOU REALLY *ENJOY* DOING.

take as much effort to roll it downhill and watch it pick up steam.

Working smart means looking for snowballs that are already near the top of the mountain, only requiring a little effort to gain the movement that turns to momentum. It may be the partner that provides the abilities that you don't possess in order to get things going. It could be the venture capital that funds fast-tracking your product to market. Or it could be that someone else rolled that snowball uphill, giving up before they made it to the top, and now you've got an easy entry point to take it the rest of the way.

As I've reverse engineered my successes, I see this approach working again and again. If it takes so little effort to move mountains (or roll massive snowballs down a mountain), you might wonder what you will do with the rest of your time.

DON'T FEAR FREE TIME

In a world where busyness is something to be admired and hard work something to be respected, whatever the results, it's not surprising that people are afraid of free time. Those leisure hours produce guilt. We feel that we're stealing time that we should be using to provide for our family or build our dreams.

We also fear the search for something to put in that time. If work is your life, then it can become a mechanism for avoiding other life issues that need tending—a spouse, children, other family problems. We need that free time in order to take a good hard look at the challenges in our lives.

And achieving results from little effort *feels* wrong! We're so used to the idea that rewards only come from hard work, that if we make a six-figure deal after outsourcing the hard stuff and sending a few emails, it feels unfair.

But that feeling is out of date. My great-grandfather was an architect in Chicago—a building he designed on Dearborn Street is on the city's historic register—and during the Depression he saw the lines of people with nothing to do. He saw the unemployed sitting on street corners wishing they had work to fill their time. For him, a fulfilling life was a life filled with work and activity, and that was the message he spread to the next generation. My father became an architect, and so did his brother.

That was a time when the number of hours someone worked determined what they could earn because more people were paid by the hour. We're now in a different time—an entrepreneurial age. Certainly there will be times when you have to "hustle." Open a new restaurant, and you'll be putting in long hours at the beginning. There are seasons when long hours are necessary. But at some point, even that restaurateur will have to step back, hire a chef, and trust someone to manage the restaurant while they reap the profits and look for a place to open a second location. The alternative is high blood pressure, exhaustion, and broken relationships.

Today, something that sounds too good can still be true. In this day and age, you really can just send a few emails. And if they are the right emails, sent to the right person at the right time—if you get your leverage just right—you *can* close the big deal. Back when I was young and selling *Encyclopedia*

Britannica in the Dallas area, I spent six weeks calling leads and meeting with prospects with absolutely nothing to show for it. I was just about ready to throw in the towel. My manager believed in me and suggested I take some leads for a remote area in east Texas and spend the weekend attempting to secure meetings. I came back from that weekend with four orders and a sizeable commission!

Now, much of that success is a numbers game. The old idea that the more people you call, the better your chances of making sales remains true, but not in quite the same way. Today's data economy means that we now know exactly *who* we should contact. Busyness no longer equals productivity. Smartness produces results—and you can be smart by yourself.

GO SOLO AND SMART

After a number of years building a team with a few dozen employees, I am now happily a "solopreneur" once again. While we developed some fantastic products and services, I learned the hard way that having a large organization just wasn't for me. For some people it's great, but I don't need to lead a team of people. I am much happier now being the only salaried person on my payroll and outsourcing contractors to do whatever I need done. I work fewer hours, and while it means I walk away from opportunities that I just don't have the time to take up, I enjoy a much higher quality of life.

Michael O'Neal, host and producer of the popular *Solopreneur Hour* podcast, has talked about leaving as much as

$200,000 on the table by choosing instead to wake up when he wants to, walk down to his favorite coffee shop, and schedule his day the way he wants. He might be able to hire people to take those opportunities if he wanted to, but he doesn't. He has a good life, the life he enjoys, and he doesn't need any more. Working more hours and employing a team might bring him more income, but it would take him away from the life he wants to live.

Being a solopreneur means that you are the boss and the buck stops with you. It doesn't mean that you're a business failure. It doesn't mean that you're incapable of growing your business. It means that the business *you* want to lead is small and agile. It means that you can take opportunities as they arise. I've discovered that the more organic the unfolding of my businesses, the more likely I am to succeed in them and have a happier life along the way. If someone were to ask me my ten-year plan or even my five-year plan, I'd have to laugh. I don't have a problem with those who set long-term goals; it's just that I prefer to leave my options open. And the old adage has some truth to it: "The best-laid plans of mice and men often go awry."

There are things on my calendar and projects that I am working through, but a year is all I can see ahead, and it's all I need to see. I know there will be surprises. I know there will be opportunities. And as a solopreneur, I know that I'll be nimble enough to make the most of them. It's much easier to turn a speedboat with one person aboard than an aircraft carrier that holds thousands. It's much easier, too, to get out of trouble. Downsizing from thirty-eight people was difficult and took a long time, but now if I'm not comfortable with how a venture is developing, I can change direction easily.

The alternative is to find that you're trapped. You have responsibilities to yourself and to your employees that you can't walk away from. You work hard because that's what's expected, and because in your current situation it's the only way to meet those responsibilities. You make excuses and say that there is no way out, but there is always a way out. The change might be hard, but the benefit is the freedom to do what you want when you want where you want with the people you want and for the reasons you want. Within the confines of our life on earth, we are empowered to master our own universe, and we get to dream and do what we want with our lives. That freedom can make us more productive.

I don't want to make it sound like I'm encouraging people to fire anybody. I'm not. And I'm not saying that building a team is bad. If that is fun for you and that is where your passion lies, then go for it. But a lot of people aren't made that way and have been made to believe that that is the *only* way.

I was lucky. My first major deal came relatively easily. It didn't come as the result of no work at all, but I've worked harder at other projects and received much less. It taught me that you can have fun and achieve huge results when you work in a way that resonates with who you really are.

⇒ 6 ⇐

KEEPING IT REAL

Lou Mongello looks the part. He's a stocky guy with a big voice, and if he told you that he was a lawyer from New Jersey, you would have no problem believing him.

You would be wrong. Lou *did* practice law in New Jersey. But that was what he did, not who he is. The person he has always been—and the person he is now—is one of the world's biggest Disney World fans. Lou was one of the first to visit Walt Disney World back in 1971, and in 2003 he set himself the challenge of writing a book about the theme park. The book grew into a website, then a podcast, then after quitting his law practice and moving his family to

Florida, a full-time business that allows Lou to visit Disney parks, write and broadcast about the rides and the restaurants, and give talks to entrepreneurs about starting their own businesses.

"I practiced law because I wanted to help people," he says. "But it wasn't in my DNA. It wasn't what I was supposed to be doing. I didn't get up every day smiling and looking forward to the day ahead, and since I made that change, that is what every day is like for me."

(Lou personifies the subject of this book. That's why I asked him to pen the foreword! Did you catch that?)

We are made to be who we are, and being anything other than who we are means being fake. Authenticity brings us back from phoniness. We see that phoniness all the time. When we turn on the TV, we see sitcoms in which every problem is solved in twenty-two minutes with eight commercials. That's not how life works. But these are the models that we're given—models of how we're supposed to look, of ideal perfectionism, beauty, and intelligence. If you want to succeed, you need to look this way, act this way, dress this way, behave this way, join this group.

All the messages we're bombarded with tell us that if we are like that person or that group, then we're good. We'll be successful and loved and accepted. Those are false messages. That's not how the real world works.

In an era filled with so many false messages, what we're looking for is real human connection: real honesty, warts and all.

AUTHENTICITY BRINGS US BACK FROM PHONINESS.

FAILURE IS AUTHENTIC

We've all made mistakes. We've all fallen down. You might say it's in our DNA. There's nobody that hasn't experienced failure. I wouldn't be where I am now without having fallen down and gotten scrapes—many of them. If you're going to swing for the fences, you've got to swing, which means you're going to strike out a lot. Babe Ruth struck out way more times than he hit home runs, but he was still the home-run king of his era. Sometimes you hit it out of the park. Sometimes you miss. And sometimes you end up on base with a single. You don't know what will happen until you pick up the bat, and there's no shame in swinging and missing.

Authenticity allows us to talk about those swings and misses, and we *should* talk about them. The most inspirational stories contain elements of failure, because we can all identify with failure. When people who are struggling to get their business off the ground hear you talk about your business idea that went south, they think: "Hey, if this person can flop, then that gives us hope."

I have plenty of those stories! Back when Budweiser did its "Whassup" commercials, I figured that phrase was going to be so hot. So I built an online greeting card site that allowed people to send a cartoon of a celebrity doing an animated whassup. It was called Virtual-Whassup.com, and I really thought I was on to something.

It was horrible. It bombed. I keep it running today as a testament to one of my failures. Go ahead and check it out. You can have a great laugh at my expense.

It didn't stop me from trying again though. Around 2009 my team convinced me to build a mobile marketing platform that would send autoresponders to mobile devices. (It's the same concept as subscribing to an email list and having a series of emails sent your way.) I put six figures into building up a service and creating a team. We went to industry events and rented booths. We promoted it hard.

It failed miserably. We got a handful of clients and spent a whole lot of money. When I realized that I wasn't going to succeed on my own, I tried to find a partner. Then I tried to find capital, and when I couldn't get capital, I tried to sell it to somebody who would know what to do with it. And I realized that that wasn't going to happen either.

Finally, I had to make a difficult decision. If I pulled the plug, the code would be worthless. The technology was all attached to one system and needed to be constantly maintained. But I looked again at how much I was paying to keep the technology alive, and I made the decision to kill it.

I was really concerned that the moment I did that, I would feel like a failure. There would be no more hope for it and no coming back.

But the moment I pulled the plug, I had a very different experience. It was like a weight lifted off my shoulders. It was liberating. I felt good. I felt happy. I wasn't mourning the death of this thing or the loss of the time and resources I had put into it. And I took a valuable lesson from the experience. I realized that I stopped failing the moment I stopped paying for it. The product failed, but the decision to end it was a success. I had stopped the bleeding, as well as the albatross that thing had become, and was now free to move on to other things.

Failure is always with us, and it's a beautiful thing—something to embrace and share, not hide and ignore. It's real, and owning it is part of what makes you authentic.

WHEN AUTHENTICITY BECOMES A CONFESSION

There is a difference, though, between being authentic and being too open. In general, today we see a trend toward too much openness on social media. But that's not the kind of humble authenticity I'm talking about. People think that because they can say something, they should. Because they have a platform, they have a voice, and they don't discern whether that platform matches what they want to say.

People going through the heat of a relationship breakup, for example, should do nothing more than be in touch with close family or friends—people who love them and can support them. They don't need to go on Facebook and tell the world. The same is true in business. It's always best to be most transparent with those who are closest to us, those that matter most. In business, that's going to be your team. You don't have to go out to the whole world and declare that your business is struggling. You'll just make sure that it continues to struggle through the problems until they are resolved.

One result of authenticity is that it opens the space for other people to talk and find support. It's like people struggling with addiction. They want to hear from other people who have been through the same battles, and they want to be able to talk without fear, judgment, or reprisal. The more we create safe venues for people to be fully human, honest, and authentic, the better.

The process starts at the hardest point: with being honest with yourself. There's a reason that self-actualization is at the top of Maslow's hierarchy of needs: it takes time and experience. Knowing yourself, really being honest with yourself, takes a lot of courage.

It's much easier to see the flaws in others and to give other people advice. We love to tell others what they should and shouldn't do. We're so good at it. But asking ourselves the tough questions of life, knowing ourselves well enough to understand our strengths and our weaknesses (especially the weaknesses)—that's tough! When we have the courage to take inventory of ourselves and identify what we're not happy about, to change and build a life that matches who we really are, that's the real challenge.

When I suggest authenticity as a preferred model for communication, please know that I put my money where my mouth is. In the summer of 2015, I was invited to deliver a TED Talk in Denver at TEDxMileHigh. In front of an audience of 2,200 people at the historic Ellie Caulkins Opera House in downtown Denver, I opened my talk on authenticity and transparency with a bold confession.

I shared how my wife of twenty-three years left me and that I struggled with numerous addictions in my life. You could have heard a pin drop. Instead I just heard the beating of my own heart as the words left my mouth.

You see, my message would have been a bee without a stinger if I had not taken the first steps to demonstrate how openness and truth bond us together as human beings. When someone shares their struggles, it creates a safe space for others to do likewise. We realize that we are not alone and that it's okay to keep it real.

The talk, entitled "Being Human in the Digital Age," encouraged the audience to approach social media thoughtfully, recognizing that being wise requires thinking through how others will feel and react before making a post.

MATCH YOUR OPPORTUNITIES
TO THE AUTHENTIC YOU

I'm often asked whether people should mix business and personal life on their profiles. I am my own brand, and I don't know how to separate myself from my work. It's all part of who I am and what I do.

It's not unusual for me to post strategies for leveraging live video for your business one day and a silly selfie of me eating delicious bacon the next. They are both part of who I am, and I prefer to provide people with an authentic picture of that reality. The truth is, my followers respond to me more when they see the more relatable, human parts of my life. I am not my business, but business is part of what I do.

Try sharing parts of your life with your followers on social media and watch your engagement increase. It makes sense because people want to connect with others they can identify with. Your business strategy might not be of particular interest to them, but a photo of the steakhouse meal you're about to carve into could be just the ticket!

If you are sharing content that matters to you, people will sense your passion.

One of the things that made it easier to pull the plug on my mobile autoresponder system was that I was never truly passionate about it. I believed in it. I believed it would help people. But it took me away from what was really in my heart.

It's easier to get sidetracked by those opportunities. People contact me regularly with all sorts of offers. In 2016 somebody contacted me about a cryptocurrency product. I'd had Bitcoin explained to me half a dozen times and I still didn't get it. The person then sent me a white paper, which looked great, but I had to tell him I was the wrong guy.

Bitcoin has since flown through the roof, and it looks to be a multibillion-dollar industry. I'm fully aware that investing could have made me a lot of money, but it just wasn't in my soul at the time. I was okay with that, but during the writing of this manuscript, my fun approach to life has dealt me a fascinating new twist.

After speaking with a friend in spring 2017, I decided to finally begin exploring the world of cryptocurrency. I became fascinated with Bitcoin and blockchain technology. As a result, I started a podcast with my friend Travis Wright, who is a marketing technologist. Called the *Bad Crypto Podcast*, the show was designed to teach newbies what we are learning as we go.

The twist isn't that I finally decided to go down the crypto rabbit hole. It's that the show has become one of the most downloaded cryptocurrency-related shows on iTunes! Now we're regularly meeting movers and shakers in the industry, being asked to attend events, and looking at ways to grow our audience. All the while we are having great fun. And if that doesn't perfectly punctuate everything I've been seeking to relate to you in this book, I don't know what does! The world of cryptocurrency finally aligned with my interests at just the right time.

Another person who has found his alignment is Croix Sather. Croix holds the world record for running across America, and he broke the world record for running across Death Valley, a feat he accomplished in 117-degree heat. He's also an author and a speaker, and his successful Kickstarter campaign to create the Dream Big life planner raised money from more than 2,500 backers. So when Croix called me up in early 2017 to tell me he was coming to Denver, I immediately asked if he needed a place to stay.

He did. In fact, Croix had been homeless for three months.

It wasn't that Croix couldn't afford a home, nor had he been evicted. He'd just chosen to spend three months on the road, traveling across America and staying with friends. Apart from a couple of work obligations, he was free to go wherever he wanted. By the time he reached my sofa, Croix had put nine thousand miles on his car, traveled from Connecticut to Florida, spent time in the Bahamas and Costa Rica, driven to California, and was on his way back to New York.

"I had grown stale," he told me. "I needed a big change. I learned that the social expectation of having one place and living there doesn't really fit me all that well. Not that I wanted to be homeless forever, but this is alignment, and the biggest lesson is to be in alignment with whoever you are."

Moving your life into alignment with your authentic self can cause problems. There are people who will be repelled by the truth, in part because they've not yet come to terms with their own truth. You could lose friends who like you for who they think you are and not who you really are. And you will win over others who will appreciate that you're being open and honest and authentic and are creating an arena to attract others who want something similar. Your authenticity gives them permission to be equally honest.

Let people who might be offended, be offended. We need to be unafraid to say what we think and share what we feel regardless of the consequences.

That doesn't mean you're completely free. There will always be things you need to do—otherwise you can't eat or pay your bills, which would be a form of self-harm. But when those tasks are in alignment with who you are, they don't feel like chores. They're not things you "should" do. They're things you choose to do. I *choose* to schedule a podcast. I *choose* to schedule an event where I've been asked to speak. I *choose* to have leisure time with a friend or family member. That's autonomy. That's freedom. That's being who I am.

There are people who believe that if they remove all those choices, if they remove entirely the need to make decisions, only then will they be in touch with their authentic selves. They sell their business, pocket the money, and retire to the beach.

And they get bored. It's not healthy. A study of 2,956 retirees by the National Institute on Aging found that healthy retirees who had worked a year longer than others over the age of sixty-five reduced their chances of dying by 11 percent. Even unhealthy people reduced their chances of dying by 9 percent if they stayed in work.[1] As Andy Dufresne said in *The Shawshank Redemption*, "Get busy living, or get busy dying."

NEVER MEET YOUR IDOLS

An old saying warns against ever meeting your heroes. But actually meeting heroes is fine. A real hero is somebody who has done something worthy of respect. Your hero might be the local firefighter who pulls on her helmet and runs into a burning building because that's her job, or the police officer who goes toe-to-toe every night with gangbangers and drug dealers, or a military veteran who has treated a colleague under fire, or even a stay-at-home mom who's raising her kids and never misses a soccer match.

Meeting your idols though? That's a whole different kettle of fish, because idols are not real. They are simply projections without flaws, weaknesses, or limitations, an image that someone—or someone's PR company—wants to project. But that's not reality. Brad Pitt might have people to take out his trash for him, but he still makes trash—and until it goes out, it still stinks up his kitchen just like everyone else's. So don't mistake an image for reality.

Sometimes, though, if we are involved in building an image and creating a brand, we discover an authentic aspect of ourselves that we didn't know was there. Jay Baer, for example, is a digital marketing consultant and a speaker who's known for wearing loud plaid suits on stage. His tailor has pictures of all the suits he's sold Jay, and you can see a development from standard business suits to the big, standout plaids that Jay is now famous for, as he became more comfortable wearing them. The reason Jay wears them, even though offstage he's more likely to wear slacks and a black turtleneck, is that he found it helps him to stay loose and be his authentic self on stage. "Authenticity connects with audiences in a way that polish cannot," he says.

We can look at what made the people we admire who they are. We can learn what they did and we can emulate their techniques. But ultimately, we have to discover who we are in order to bring to those techniques our own authentic selves. When we do that, we get to live in our own personal Disney Worlds.

~~~~~~~~~~~~~~~~~~~~~~~~

FUN IS ON THE OTHER SIDE OF FEAR

Rachel Martin knows all about joy. You'd think that she wouldn't have time. A professional blogger and single mom of seven children (count them!), she's known days of whirlwind emergencies, searches for lost homework, unending board games, and laundry mountains so high you'd need a Sherpa to reach the summit.

But while writing her blog *FindingJoy.net*, she's found not only a way to build a business that gives her fulfillment but also sources of fun in places she would never have thought to look.

One strange discovery came when she moved from Minnesota to Nashville. Rachel rented a twenty-six-foot truck, packed everything she owned into the back, then drove the truck herself 935 miles across the country. "With the wind gusting up to forty miles an hour, I drove this beast of a truck terrified," she recalls. "But as the day went on, I started to enjoy this very thing I was terrified of."

Rachel found herself having so much fun that as she passed the truck stops in Illinois, she'd wave at the other drivers sitting in the cabs of their ten-tonners.

Rachel started the day in fear, but having faced that fear, she ended it enjoying the fun of the very thing that had scared her most.

Rachel is unlikely to get behind the wheel of a twenty-six-foot truck again, but she is going to be running regularly. That might not sound like much, but it's also an activity that Rachel didn't think she would ever enjoy.

"I thought I couldn't do it," she says. "I told myself I can't run. I'm only a team sport person. I'll quit."

But once she'd arrived in Nashville, she found her excuse that it was too cold to run just didn't fly anymore. "The little lie I told myself was really just something I needed to push through," she says. "And in pushing through it, I discovered it was something I really loved. I put my headphones on, and for thirty-seven minutes, I have the world to myself."

Rachel says that she lives according to Eleanor Roosevelt's maxim to "do one thing every day that scares you." It might be something as small as ordering a different drink at Starbucks, but it could also be as large as changing hair color or taking up what looks like an impossible challenge.

It might not always work. Picking up a spider might be something you fear, but it's unlikely to be something you enjoy. But many of the things you might find fun—whether it's driving a vehicle with a powerful engine, taking up a sport, or running your own business—lie on the other side of fear. The pro cess starts with a sense of nerves and a truckload of caution. But, gradually, you find your speed, you start to enjoy the journey, and eventually you get a kick out of waving at the other people on the road. You're up, running, and having fun.

⇒ 7 ⇐

SAY YES TO SERENDIPITY

Sue B. Zimmerman used to run art classes for children.
The kids would come to her home, she'd lay out the paper
and the scissors and the glue, and the kids would go at it.
They'd have a great time and go home with sticky fingers and
clumped hair and paint all over their clothes. Sue would then
have to scrape sticky stuff off her kitchen table.

One day, a friend turned up with an alternative. Instead
of glue, she brought a roll of toupee tape—the tape men use to
stick hairpieces to their heads.

The kids had a ball. They decorated the tape and cut it
and played with it, and they did it all without making a mess.

Sue saw the opportunity. She took the tape, decorated it

herself, and marketed it to scrapbook enthusiasts as Treasure Tape. You could still use it to stick your wig to your head, but now it was also pretty and you could decorate your photo album with it. The tape was sold in craft chains Michaels and AC Moore, and Sue presented it twice on the QVC shopping channel.

The business didn't last long. The lack of a patent and low-cost Chinese competition soon wiped it out. But while it lasted, it was a good business, and it all came down to the serendipity of a friend and some spare toupee tape.

Being observant and receptive to what is happening around you opens you up to new opportunities. The biggest triumph can come in small unexpected packages, but you have to fine-tune your spidey senses to recognize them.

We all have moments of serendipity. We all have flashes of blinding good fortune that change our direction and send us off in wonderful new directions, if we are willing to follow our gut instinct and take action.

MOMENT OF SERENDIPITY OR LONG-TERM DISTRACTION?

Not all serendipity is as valuable as it might look at first. Sometimes that glint on the pavement is just a gum wrapper, not a lost diamond ring. The ability to tell the difference between serendipity and a time-waster becomes more finely tuned the older we become. We learn—or should learn— from experience, from trial and error, and from remembering when we've been taken off course before. It comes from being in alignment with who we are and what we want. It's that awareness that allows us to turn down opportunities that look good and promise much but don't match what we really want.

Until you have that awareness, though (and it only comes with time), you have to analyze the opportunity and trust your gut. Gut feelings go to the core of who we are. If your gut is telling you that something is not quite right, it's worth listening to it. Now, that feeling could just be fear, but more often it's a warning. At times I haven't listened to that warning and I've started down paths that weren't right for me, even though I knew deep down that the way I was going wasn't right.

But the opposite has happened too. Other times people have told me, "This isn't right for you," but I believed it was and I stuck with it, and it worked.

You have to learn to trust yourself, and that can be difficult, especially if you were raised in a family where you weren't encouraged to make your own decisions or had siblings or peers who put you down. When that happens, you don't learn to trust your own decision-making process. But those gut feelings are important. They should not be the basis for everything you do, but they are a great starting point.

And if your gut tells you, "This intrigues me. This interests me," and that interest is not about the money at stake but the subject, the topic, the product, or the service, that's a great sign.

You have to keep listening though. A process isn't just made up of milestones. It's a daily reevaluation of what you're doing to make sure it feels, looks, smells, sounds, and tastes right. The moment one of those senses doesn't quite resonate with the others, there's a temptation to rationalize, to declare that you're a true believer and are going to persist. That failure to read the signs has been the downfall of many businesses. But when something resonates with you and keeps resonating with you, it doesn't matter whether or not it ends up being profitable; if you enjoy the process, it will be a life success. You will learn something from it. Those building blocks take you one step closer to the alignment and fulfillment you're seeking.

ENGINEERING SERENDIPITY

Serendipity can arrive out of nowhere, but it usually happens when the groundwork has already been done. You can't engineer serendipity, but you can create an environment that lends itself to things happening. I don't believe in accidents, and I don't believe in luck. I believe there's a reason things happen in our lives, and those things happen when preparation meets opportunity. I call it "showing up."

Showing up at events, for example, has opened up all sorts of new opportunities for me. If I hadn't been at a conference in 2004, seen someone's AdSense earnings on their screen, and realized that Google really had something for publishers, I wouldn't have discovered the keys to generating a fantastic passive income and passed my knowledge on to others via my book *The AdSense Code*. That was good "luck," but it only

YOU CAN'T
ENGINEER
SERENDIPITY, BUT
YOU CAN CREATE
AN ENVIRONMENT
THAT LENDS
ITSELF TO THINGS
HAPPENING.

happened because I was there, doing something I enjoyed, and open to doing something else that looked fun.

When you show up, when you're there, you connect with people—and you never know who you're going to meet. You never know how you're going to be able to help that person or how they'll be able to help you in the future. I've met people at events and partnered with them on important deals ten years later. That would never have happened if I hadn't attended that conference and if that person had not thought, *I think I'll just go and see what this event is all about*, and struck up a conversation with me in a hallway.

For years we've talked about six degrees of separation between people, but it's more like two to three now because of the internet. We're all so connected that if there's somebody you want to meet, you probably know somebody who knows somebody who knows them, especially if you're on Facebook and LinkedIn.

The connections you make don't have to lead to a new business opportunity either. They can just enrich your life. For all the spread of dating sites and Tinder-like apps, the story of many marriages is still just the story of serendipity. You accept that dinner party invitation, agree to meet friends for a drink, and you meet the love of your life.

I've built some great business relationships attending events and conferences, but I've made far more friends who have made my life more fulfilling and fun than it's ever been.

And of course, we get to spread that joy too. When we make ourselves available for serendipitous meetings, we get to connect the people we meet. You'll see that in one circle you have somebody who would really benefit from meeting that person in another circle. It takes seconds to open Facebook, create a message between them, and make the introduction. You don't even have to tell them why. Part of the fun is giving them the chance to figure it out for themselves. I'll often connect two people by messaging them both and saying, "Jane, you should meet Joe. Joe, Jane is someone you should speak to. Trust me on this. Have fun!" and leave them to it. They'll figure it out, and they'll share an experience when they do. It's unscripted connecting, and it makes their connection much more authentic. In fact, it's one of my favorite things to do! As someone who seeks to exert minimum effort for maximum effect, I can't imagine anything simpler than connecting two people and watching magical things happen.

Magic doesn't always happen, because life is unscripted and full of surprises. But often just showing up is half the victory.

⇥ 8 ⇤

WORK AND PLAY ARE
MADE TO GO TOGETHER

For some of us, fun comes easily. For others, not so much. Some people are by nature more serious, more analytical and methodical. But as kids, most of us just wanted to play. Few children need to be told to go and have fun. They're curious and imaginative, so if they don't have a toy, they'll find something else. Before we had computers and mobile devices, we'd go outside, gather other kids in the neighborhood, find a tin can, and kick it around.

Every kid does that, but for some people that spark of fun burns brighter and burns longer. Even so, society is pretty good at blowing out that light. We go to school to learn a little bit of this and a little bit of that. In college things get more serious, and then along comes work. I've watched my own kids cope with the gravity of becoming young adults: paying for their own places and utilities and food and clothing and insurance. It's not easy—and there's something to be said for not becoming an adult—but we have to do it. The question is *how* we do it. I choose to live playfully and be curious and interested in things that are interesting to me. (This is one reason you'll find me at music concerts, especially living in Denver where we have Red Rocks Amphitheatre, arguably the coolest place to see a show in the United States.)

I brought this same playfulness into my business when I had a team of developers, designers, administrators, salespeople, and managers working for me.

Around 2005 I discovered the flying slingshot monkey. Essentially, it's a stuffed toy with rubber bands that attach the arms to the body. By placing your forefinger and pinky finger into the hands and pulling back on the legs, then releasing, you send the masked and caped primate through the air to its destination, accompanied by a flying monkey screech as it soars like a bird. I immediately fell in love with this toy.

When I saw my team getting overworked, I decided it was time to bring the workday to a halt and conduct the Flying Monkey Office Olympics!

Every team member was given a monkey and told to decorate the black cape with a symbol representing them. Fortunately, we had Wite-Out on hand to bring art to life.

Each person was then invited to compete in three different events: Monkey Bowling, Trash Monkey, and Flight of the Monkey. We added up points and awarded trophies to the winning monkeys. If you'd like to see it, there's a video on YouTube. Just search for "flying monkey office Olympics."

To this day, the flying monkey is my mascot. Whenever I speak, I'll often fling a monkey from the stage so the audience knows we are going to have a good time.

What is the point of this? Fun. Pure, playful, childlike fun.

Debra Lee is an attorney who left her legal practice and joined a start-up television network. She became the CEO of the now-successful Black Entertainment Television (BET) network. In an interview with the Stanford School of Business, Lee summed up her reason for making the leap from high-paying career to risky and uncertain future by saying, "I'm just not having fun anymore. I think work should be fun."[1]

LAUGHTER IS ESSENTIAL

One of the reasons we lose our sense of playfulness is that we try to protect ourselves from being seen as we really are: a human being who is beautiful and wonderful, but also beautifully and wonderfully flawed and frail. We make mistakes and shame kicks in. We fall down and we're embarrassed.

But when somebody falls down with style and gets right up with a big "tada!" like they meant to do it, it's funny.

I often get on stage or do a live video that's unscripted. I'll have a general sense of what I want to discuss, but because

I'm not following a script I'll often put my foot in my mouth. When I do, I'll stop and slap my head, then turn to the audience and say, "Did I just say that? I really just said that, didn't I?" It's real, and people like it. They relate to people who are unafraid to laugh at themselves. There are a thousand things in the world that we have no control over, from disease to disaster, but there's something about not taking ourselves seriously and laughing at our own humanity.

During the summer of 2008 I was involved in a project that did exactly that.

Steve Jobs had just announced that Apple would begin allowing third-party developers to distribute the company's apps through the iTunes App Store. As an early adopter of the iPhone, I was delighted. I pulled my team into the conference room, and we began filling the whiteboard with ideas for apps. We didn't know just how big the iPhone would become, but we knew that being a part of this explosive industry was something we wanted to do.

Many ideas sprang from that exciting brainstorming session, including an app called iVote Mobile, which was one of the first one thousand apps released to the App Store.

Then, a couple of months later, the big idea hit us.

Now I'll need you to cut me slack here because what I'm about to share with you is a little, shall we say, unorthodox.

Someone on my team joked that it would be funny to create a novelty app that would simulate sounds. Well, there's no easy way to say this so I'll just spit it out.

The app would simulate flatulence. Fart sounds. The name? iFart Mobile.

You may have heard of it because it grabbed headlines around the world when it was released in December 2008. The app skyrocketed to number one in the App Store and reigned there for more than three weeks!

(This is the part where I drag out the puns, so prepare to groan.)

The app was explosive. Some said it was a gas. It was so popular we made quite a stink. And there's plenty more hot air to this story.

While we anticipated some would enjoy the app and we suspected we'd make some profits from it, we never imagined it would become famous, even infamous. Suddenly, iFart and my name were featured in news articles, blogs, and social media posts around the world.

Kathie Lee Gifford demonstrated the app on *The Today Show*, ending her post-demonstration laughter with, "That starts my day off so happy. I love that!"

Lance Armstrong tweeted that he was pranking a dinner guest with the app. The guest was none other than Robin Williams. (I confess, it makes me smile to know that I created something that made one of the greatest comedians of our time laugh.)

The *New York Times* did a Sunday magazine full-page story titled "Dumb and Dumber 2.0," lamenting a culture in which an app as banal as iFart could rise to the top of the charts.

Needless to say, the journey was great fun. If you would have told teenage Joel that farting would one day become profitable, he would have thought you were insane. Or a genius. Or both.

I took a risk on something and let the rest unfold. The result was a success story that still follows me to this day. Occasionally the app gets mentioned in a book or article and the inevitable requests to share my story surface once again. Who knew farts could get so much mileage?

There may be some reading this who would feign disgust. But when I have the opportunity to take the stage and share this story, invariably the audience wants me to do a live demonstration. I gladly take out the app, and the crowd shrieks with delight.

While there isn't a digital methane meter to let us know just how many fart sounds have been released into the atmosphere, our estimates put it at more than one billion. That's a lot of laughter from a simple app that took a risk.

I fully realize that in spite of my other accomplishments, my tombstone could very well say "iFarted." So go ahead. Laugh at fart sounds. If you snort when you laugh, do it with reckless abandon. And then laugh at yourself for having laugh-snorted. It's all good.

A THOUSAND FLAVORS OF FUN

What we enjoy varies tremendously. Each individual defines fun differently. Some people love to code. For them, hunkering down at their workstation with Mountain Dew and a bag of Doritos to pound out JavaScript all day is great fun. Some people love numbers. While being an actuary or an accountant sounds like hell to me, some people like it. There are plenty of people who love making music or other art regardless of whether somebody will buy it or even hear or see it. They just want to create it. Until someone tells us to choose a profession, we have a tendency to gravitate toward that which interests us the most—and what interests us the most is what will give us the most fun. It's how we live our lives in a way that is authentic and true to who we are and want to be.

To find those interests, we have to experiment. Trying new things is a key to discovery, a way to learn more about ourselves and about others. Between 2011 and 2013 I took a sabbatical. I was going through a difficult period in my personal life and in my business life, and I needed to pull back from everything. That was when I slowly let go of my entire staff and went back to being a solopreneur. I stopped writing books. I wasn't doing any speaking. And on social media I was present, but not constantly. I took the time to work on myself physically; I lost a lot of weight. Emotionally, I dealt with a lot of baggage, and spiritually, I reconnected with God in a way that I hadn't done in a long time. It was a really challenging yet enriching time for me.

In late 2012 I knew I wasn't quite ready to get back to what I had been doing previously, but I also needed to expand my horizons.

I asked myself what would shake my paradigm most. *I know, I'll get a job!*

I didn't *need* a job. But I was curious to see how I would function as an employee after so many years of being self-employed.

I knew I couldn't work in a restaurant because I'd be terrible. I'd drop food and get orders wrong and eat all the

TRYING NEW THINGS IS A KEY TO DISCOVERY, A WAY TO LEARN MORE ABOUT OURSELVES AND ABOUT OTHERS.

desserts. I thought about being a blue shirt at an electronics store, but I figured I would get tired of asking people all day long whether they were finding everything okay. So I ended up in the only place right for an author: a bookstore. I went to the local Barnes and Noble, and I asked for a job application.

The manager came out. He read the application, looked up at me, and said: "What are you doing here?" After all, I am a *New York Times* bestselling author, and my books appeared on their store shelves.

I explained to him that I love books, wanted to do something different, and being on the other side of the cash register would be a really interesting experience. We skipped the three-stage interview process and five minutes later, he put out his hand and said, "You're hired."

So I started putting the books on the shelves and making sure they were all arranged at the end of the day—and I worked at the cash register. And it was such a great experience! When people came to the cash register, I talked to them. I would look at the books they were buying and have a conversation. These conversations were interesting for me because you never knew who you're going to meet. And they were great for the store because they allowed me to sell memberships to the store's loyalty program. I ended up selling more memberships to the loyalty program than any other cashier in the store at that time, simply because I was doing what I enjoyed: talking to people about their books.

This didn't create a new career path for me, but as an author it was incredibly useful to stand on the other side of the counter and experience the book industry from that perspective.

Not all work-related endeavors redirect us in our profession. But just as a house is built brick upon brick, our life experiences shape who we are becoming and how we engage with others.

Sometimes taking these kinds of risks just because they sound fun and interesting leads to new opportunities. Sometimes they just make for great stories. I see both as valuable.

I'm a big fan of Uber, and I wondered what it would be like to be an Uber driver. I drive a two-door Mustang, so I couldn't use my car, but I borrowed my son's four-door. I mounted a GoPro camera on the dashboard and filmed myself driving for Uber. I drove around for a week, took a lot of people for rides, and documented the whole thing. I told them what I was doing, asked them about their experiences with Uber, and ended up making a short film about it and posting it on YouTube. It shows the other side of the Uber experience. I got out and engaged with people. If Uber allowed two-doors, I'd probably still be doing it sometimes.

Some of the results of that experimentation were a much better understanding of myself and the chance to develop a much deeper degree of empathy. Some people have that naturally, but for me, it's been part of the process of my own successes and failures. As I've started over and participated in activities that have put me in unusual situations, I've also developed a much deeper understanding of others.

So we shouldn't be afraid to try something new. If you're in a rut and keep doing the same thing, you're going to stay in that rut. Think about what you like to do. If you like playing music, then maybe put an ad on Craigslist to see who needs a bass player or a kazoo player or whatever it is that you play. Look for meetups in your area. Even if there's not something in your field, try something different. Take a camera and join the photography meetup. Do something! The trap people get into is they don't do anything because they don't feel empowered to make a change. They just stay on the sofa.

Change starts with a decision, but that decision is hard to make because change is scary and unpredictable. We have hopes and dreams and our own built-in expectations of what we think is going to take place, but things rarely turn out the way we imagine them. Life has a way of throwing us all kinds of curveballs, for better or for worse. The challenge isn't to avoid them. It's to be joyful as they come toward us, to remain grounded in our behavior and actions when our emotions are screaming everything to the contrary. That's a true sign of maturity. Greater personal fulfillment and joy are the result.

TRAVEL WITH SHEILA

I learned a lot about the joy that curiosity can bring from my mother. My mom has always had a hunger for seeing the world. It was because of her that my horizons were broadened as a child. She took us to Europe, the Caribbean, South America, and all over the United States. She's now a seasoned world traveler with millions of miles under her belt. She and my stepfather have been on every continent. They're on the move about six months each year, riding elephants in India or camels in the desert. She even literally got lost in Siberia once. She loves it. She's seventy-six years old.

Twelve years ago, Mom wanted to share her stories, so I encouraged her to start a blog called Travelswithsheila.com. She did just that, and now she writes about her experiences and seeks to inspire others to go and see the world and to do so on a budget so that anyone can rack up the miles. She took a class on Final Cut Pro and learned how to edit her own videos. She now has more than 2,500 videos on her YouTube channel with more than eighteen million views. Her little blog now has a global audience, and she monetizes it with advertisements. She's a perfect example of how following your passion can lead to getting paid.

It's really not that hard to find what you enjoy. Even if fun doesn't come easily to you, even if it's been beaten out of you by school and peers, you do have something that you find fun. You might need to experiment to rediscover it, but you'll enjoy the process and you'll be on your way to turning a hobby into a profession. And that's the subject of the next chapter.

FUN HAS NO AGE

Children may need to be told to clean up their bedrooms, but they don't have to be told to have fun. Nor do they need to be told *how* to have fun. Leave them alone in a room with a stick and a bedsheet, and you'll find that they've created an entire world that can keep them amused for hours. (Leave them alone in a room with an Xbox, and you'll never see them again.)

But the fun that people of all ages enjoy varies tremendously. I'm in my fifties, and I still enjoy video games as much as I did when I was a teenager. I might not put in as many hours as I did then, but I still find them fun and love unwinding with a game at my PC.

For fifteen-year-old Caleb Maddix, fun takes a very different form. He might enjoy riding a skateboard with his friends and playing the odd video game, but his biggest pleasure is work. He's building his own speaking business, writing books that inspire other children to set and achieve goals, and building a following on social media that's already shot through six figures. By the time he was fourteen, he had shared stages with Tony Robbins, Gary Vaynerchuk, Kevin Harrington, and Jack Canfield.

None of that came as a result of nagging, allowance bribes, or threats of grounding. "I've always been an entrepreneur," he says. "My dad was a speaker and I traveled with him. I would meet other kids and none of them knew what they wanted to do."

When he was just twelve, Caleb asked his father if he could speak on stage. Then he wrote his own book and started pushing out content on social media. "It blew up," he recalls.

His first business was called "Kids with a Mission" and focused on bringing children together to help the homeless. He's since created an entire mentorship program that produces monthly content to help children set goals, find discipline, and communicate with their families.

He's well paid for those efforts. At fourteen, when his friends were washing cars and cutting lawns for dimes, Caleb was earning the kind of six-figure salary that's the envy of grown-ups. But what motivates him isn't the chance to put dollars into a bank account that he's not going to need for years. It's the chance to help other children and to enjoy the act of being an entrepreneur.

"Things that you truly prioritize, you're going to put into your schedule," he says. "My business is a priority. My friends are a priority. I need those relationships, so I make it happen. Because it's all a priority, I make it happen."

As for the state of his bedroom . . . that's not such a priority.

$\rightarrowtail 9 \leftarrowtail$

HOBBIES CAN BECOME
CAREERS—AND OFTEN DO

When I was a kid, there were no playlists or Spotify, and even MTV had yet to make its mark. If you wanted to know what the bestselling records were, you had to listen to the Top 40 on AM radio. I loved it. I'd buy 45s and LPs and play them on the record player in my room. But I also had a little tape recorder that had an external speaker, so I'd run the speaker downstairs, hit record and play on the tape recorder, and entertain the rest of the house with my selections.

I was playing DJ and having a ball, but I never thought of doing it professionally. It was just a bit of fun.

It wasn't until I was in college, between my sophomore and junior years, that a family member suggested I consider applying for a job at the college radio station. I auditioned, landed a spot on the FM station in college, and worked in nightclubs. After I graduated, my first job was as a nightclub DJ, and it led to my first entrepreneurial adventure as a mobile DJ. It all came from the natural passion I had for music.

I did the same thing a few years later when I launched WorldVillage.com, my first website. The site's first content was drawn from the *Dallas Fort Worth Software Review,* a tiny publication that I'd created solely to land free software from game companies. The system worked so well that I couldn't review everything by myself.

So I put a message on America Online (do you have any of those free floppy disks sitting in the attic?) announcing that I was looking for software reviewers. I made it clear that I couldn't afford to pay anything but I'd send the reviewer software for free. They could keep it and send me back a review. About fifty people took me up on the offer, giving me my first outsourcing experience and my first joint venture.

What I was doing in both those instances was taking something I loved and building a career. I was turning a hobby into a profession.

KNOW WHERE YOUR TALENTS LIE

I don't know if I was any good at reviewing software, but I think I made a pretty good DJ. People told me that I did a good job, and I could see that the dance floor was always full. But that doesn't always happen. People don't always know themselves well enough to know what they're good at. The people around us often see things that we don't see in ourselves, and it can take that feedback to completely change our trajectory.

If you're not sure what you want to do or where your talents lie, it's a great idea to go to somebody who knows you, whether it's a family member, a friend, or a business associate, and ask them what they think you're good at. Those opinions can be a lot more revealing than academic tests. I remember taking aptitude tests when I was in high school, and the results I received had no relation to anything that interested me.

Those areas of talent and interest can become a business. People now make money doing all kinds of things. Mieshelle Nagelschneider earns $250 an hour as a Harvard-educated . . . cat trainer. If your cat has a compulsive disorder or doesn't quite aim at the litterbox, she'll put it on the sofa and listen to its problems. You can even find cat trainers who'll teach your cat to use the toilet instead of the sand.

So dismiss nothing. Don't assume that there's something you can't make money doing. If all you like to do is sit on the sofa and watch TV, then guess what? There's TheFutonCritic. com. You can make up your own thing, write it, podcast it, or even broadcast it live. *Mystery Science Theater 3000* was a show in which a guy and his robot buddies watched old movies and commented on them. It ran right through the nineties and has now made a comeback on Netflix.

Make a list of everything you like to do and are passionate about. Don't assume that you have to know more than everyone else. It doesn't take much knowledge in any one discipline to know more than most people, because we are all masters of very little. Some of us know a little about a lot, and all of us know a lot about something. We might not know the most, but we do know more than most people, whether it's about origami, bonsai growing, or jujitsu. Jay Baer knows everything worth knowing about digital marketing, but he's also always been keen on barbecues. He trained up and he's now a barbecue contest judge. It's not a job, but he now has professional-level knowledge.

You just have to figure out the one thing that you know more than your friends, the topic that people call you about when they need advice. I know if I wanted travel tips, for example, I'd call my world-traveling mom or Chris Guillebeau. And if I wanted to know how to do a Texas barbecue, I'd call Jay Baer. There are always topics that people call you to ask advice about.

You don't need to have some unique insight into the field. The health and fitness arena, for example, is very crowded. It seems that a book comes out almost every week with a new fad that people will follow before another one comes along. Most of these books have similar messages: eat less and move your body more (which is actually the Joel Comm weight-loss plan). But there's usually at least one distinguishing characteristic that sets it apart from all of the other fitness plans and diets—and that's the selling point.

That unique point can be scary. If nobody else is saying it, then maybe there's a good reason. But the one thing that makes you different, that scares you the most, is probably the linchpin of what you're going to talk about.

Credentials don't have anything to do with your choice either. I have a bachelor's degree in speech communications, but college taught me far more about life and partying than it did about speaking. I learned about speaking by doing it. Sure, professionals like doctors, attorneys, engineers, and nuclear physicists need to be fully trained by experts in their arena. But for many of us, that kind of training doesn't really matter. Some people rack up degrees because they went to school a lot and made learning a priority. I chose to get my master's degree in things that aren't credentialed. It doesn't make me any less qualified. And those are the things I get paid best to do. Accreditations tell us a little about somebody, but they don't tell the whole story.

HURRY UP AND WAIT

None of this means you can go from interest to fun income in one giant leap. It takes time, and it takes patience. That patience is part of trusting the process, of believing that things happen in their own time. If somebody would have told me in high school, "You can be a DJ when you go to college," I might not have been ready for that. Things happen when they are supposed to.

Plenty of people, for example, are good at photography. So they build a website, put up their photos, and pitch for jobs and licensing sales, and after six weeks nothing's happened. Their pictures haven't moved. No one's hired them to shoot their wedding. It's easy to get really excited and gung ho about a project that chimes with your interests and then dismiss it as not fun when it fails to rocket away. That's impatience. It's not trusting the process.

As long as you're moving forward, you're doing the right thing. The question, though, is what do you do during that process? Do you quit your day job and jump right in, or do you work on both at the same time and move gradually toward your interest?

I don't recommend anybody just quitting their job if putting food on the table or taking care of their family is an issue. In 1996 I quit my job completely to work full-time on the internet, but I had a little cushion because of a small angel investment in our company. Once we'd blown through that and I was left with nothing, I started wondering whether I should have jumped ship. For those who need a little bit more security, slowly transitioning, testing the waters, and building over time is not a bad option.

There's no single route to turning a hobby into a profession.

Tim Urban runs a blog called *Wait But Why*. He once wrote a post in which he laid out all the months, days, and weeks he had left in his life, assuming that he'd live to be ninety. He then did the same thing for trips to the beach, the number of Chinese dumplings he's likely to eat, and the number of times he'll get to see his parents based on the frequency with which he sees them now.[1] It was a sobering picture, and it showed just how important each day becomes. Is it worth sacrificing one of your forty-odd remaining vacations for another business meeting? Is it worth giving up weeks of doing what you love to fit in more time doing what you only endure?

AS LONG AS YOU'RE MOVING FORWARD, YOU'RE DOING THE RIGHT THING.

IMPOSTER SYNDROME

You'll know you're on the right track when you don't just start seeing success at turning your hobby into a profession but when you also feel embarrassed about that success. Impostor Syndrome, when successful people feel that they don't deserve their success and are going to be found out as frauds, is remarkably common. One study found symptoms in as many as 70 percent of respondents.[2] It's normal.

In fact, if you ever reach the point where you're so proud of yourself and what you do that you don't wonder "Why me?" you might have a problem. We're all fallible, and success for all of us depends on not just effort and choices but on the people in our lives, timing, and maybe spirituality. There's much to be said for humility and recognizing your own humanity. Treating people right comes from that humility, from recognizing our flaws and faults while not putting a heavy burden on somebody else. Even knights on white horses fall off their steeds from time to time.

The challenge is to see your own inherent value. Whenever you try something that comes from your soul and your mind, something unique, there's an opportunity to bless somebody else with it. That's true whether you're working for yourself or doing a job for someone else. You have skills and abilities that are valuable—and you can put them to use.

⇥10⇤

CHOOSE YOUR
FRIENDS WISELY

When we are seeking fun in our work, work is a healthy subset of our lives. That means healthy life principles applied to all the relationships in our lives will lead to healthier relationships in our work life.

In a number of interviews I've been the subject of over the years, I've been asked what my favorite business book is. Invariably I give an answer that the host is not expecting, because my selection isn't a business book at all. It's a personal development title called *Boundaries: When to Say Yes, How to Say No to Take Control of Your Life*, by psychologists

Henry Cloud and John Townsend. That's because I'm a big believer in proper application of healthy boundaries across all areas of my life.

In this book Cloud and Townsend recall meeting a couple who were worried about their son. He had started using drugs, had dropped out of school, and was hanging around with the wrong crowd. The couple was worried. They'd done everything they could to help, giving their son a place to live and money to live on so that he could focus on his studies and enjoy a social life. Nothing was working.

The psychologists saw the problem: the couple's son didn't have one. Every problem he had, the parents had taken on themselves. Their son was able to act irresponsibly because the consequences of that lack of responsibility fell on someone else. It was like someone who doesn't water their lawn but instead of seeing it turn brown and die, gets to see it grow and flourish because their neighbor's sprinkler lands on their property.

"A little boundary clarification would do the trick," the authors said. "You need some fences to keep his problems out of your yard and in his, where they belong."[1]

It's a hard message for a parent to hear, but relationships, even between the people who are closest to us, aren't always easy to manage.

There are people who don't have others' best interests at heart. *We* don't always have everybody's best interests at heart. Even though most people aspire to be good, to make a difference, and to impact others in a positive way, we all occasionally struggle with jealousy and envy, and the world contains even more evil things than that. Choosing who you want to spend time with and how you relate to them is essential. As the old adage goes, you can't choose your family, but you can choose your friends. You can't always choose who you work with when you're in a job, but you can choose who you spend time with.

That makes your life better and it also makes your life more successful. The better we know ourselves, the better we know how others operate, and the better we're going to do in business. That's why sales and marketing is all based on persuasion and psychology. It's by understanding human behavior, knowing what pushes our buttons and flips our switches, that commercials are able to influence us to buy. It's that fine line between persuasion and manipulation. Persuasion is an ethical act designed to help someone discover that a product, service, or idea will bring value to their lives. Manipulation is a selfish and unethical act designed to get others to do what we want them to do, whether or not it's in their best interests. We need to know where that line lies throughout our lives.

YOU END WHERE OTHERS BEGIN

If there's one outstanding lesson in *Boundaries*, it's that we need to see where we end and others begin. People have a way of becoming enmeshed in others' lives. Some become people pleasers, doing what other people believe they should do and feeling guilty if they push back and refuse to pull other

AS THE OLD ADAGE
GOES, YOU CAN'T
CHOOSE YOUR
FAMILY, BUT YOU
CAN CHOOSE
YOUR FRIENDS.

people's wagons. Other people become antisocial, refusing to recognize any boundaries and doing whatever they want, whenever they want, without any concern or regard for how it impacts others.

Somewhere in between those two extremes is a healthy balance with boundaries that teach us that we can say no.

It's the hardest word to say. We don't want to disappoint people and make them feel like we've let them down. We don't want to hurt their feelings, so we add a reason. There's always an apology and an excuse—because the excuse works. The problem is that the excuse works in the other direction too. All it takes to turn a potential no into a reluctant yes is a reason.

Psychologist Ellen Langer conducted a very simple experiment that will be familiar to anyone who's ever worked in an office. She had someone cut in line at a photocopier. The first person simply said: "Excuse me, I have five pages. May I use the Xerox machine?" That request worked 60 percent of the time.

The next person said: "Excuse me, I have five pages. May I use the Xerox machine because I'm in a rush?" Adding a good reason boosted compliance to 94 percent.

The last person said: "Excuse me, I have five pages. May I use the Xerox machine because I have to make some copies?" Compliance dropped by only 1 percent even though the reason was ridiculous. Everyone in line wanted to make copies, but just giving a reason, *any reason*, was enough to make someone give something of value—their time—to a stranger for free.[2]

Unless we have agreed to a transaction, we don't owe anybody anything. We don't help others because we have to; we help because we want to, because lending a hand to a relative in trouble or a friend in need is part of our values. When we do say yes, it's because we're responsible adults. We're caring and empathetic, and it matters.

We *want* to give from our heart. What we want to avoid is people taking from us. When we make a decision to give, we do so joyfully. When others take, we start to feel resentment, anger, and bitterness. Those feelings might be turned outward to those who are taking from us, but most often they're turned inward and are turned into self-loathing.

THE GUILT OF SUCCESS

Boundaries are particularly important for people who have achieved any kind of success. As soon as you become wealthy, or even give the appearance that you are doing better than others, it's not uncommon for other people in the family to assume you've got plenty of money, so you should buy them a car or pay off their mortgage or lend them money for their business idea. If you have a lot of money and your family members need help, it certainly wouldn't be beyond imagination to share your blessings with your family. But even in this instance you want to give because that's what's in your heart, not because someone assumed you would help.

And what you don't want to happen is to feel weighed down by a sense of obligation or to feel so blessed that you believe it's undeserved. Your ability to help others isn't an obligation to give to everyone who asks. It's an opportunity to lift others up when they need your strength. Taking that opportunity has to come from your values, not from your guilt.

I often wear my "Do Good Stuff" brand T-shirt, sporting the smiling face logo and positive message. By doing so, I open myself up to those who believe they have a right to decide what good stuff is for me. While I have great compassion for the homeless, I know that I can't give assistance to everyone who asks. One time a man asked for help and I politely declined. He retorted with, "That's not good stuff."

The guilt others attempt to place on us when we don't respond as they wish is a boundary breach. It demands that we surrender our personal freedom and liberty to the whims of others. This is unhealthy for both parties, and we need to learn to recognize when this is taking place.

The good news is that guilt goes when it's replaced by gratitude, when we are humble and recognize that what we receive from others is a gift. We might have worked hard for our rewards or worked smart. We might have earned those rewards. But that's not the whole story. None of us gets to choose where we were born or the talents with which we were born. When we recognize that, we feel an urge to help, and that urge comes from a desire inside, not from a request outside.

FRIENDS WHO TAKE

Everything and everyone is either life-giving or life-taking. They either add to the experience of our lives or they drain us. Win the lottery or sell your company to Google, and you'll suddenly discover a whole bunch of new friends. When the singer MC Hammer hit it big in the eighties, he quickly found himself at the center of a large entourage that pretty much bankrupted him. While there must have been friends and family members who cared for him in the group, many weren't truly friends. They were takers who leeched off his success because there was something in it for them. That's where boundaries and discernment are really needed.

They come with time. You learn who your real friends are, the ones who stick with you through the abundant times and through the lean times. You discover who you can trust, and those people form your most intimate inner circle. My most inner circle is pretty small compared to the number of people I know, but these are the people who know me, know my life, and know what's going on—the good, the bad, and the ugly. Friends stand outside that circle. They are in your life and you value them. You know a lot about each other, but there are some things you don't share with everybody. Behind them are associates. These are the people you meet in business or in passing, at church or in the neighborhood. Beyond them are strangers, the friends you haven't met yet.

You get to choose that pecking order of relationships. You get to assign the appropriate levels of trust to each group. You can evaluate the relationship and ask whether it's balanced and fair, whether you're asking too much of each other or being a good friend. Is this a life-giving relationship or something that's draining and life-taking?

It's not just money or emotional expenditure that they

could be taking. The wrong friends can also take time—and time is the most precious commodity we have. Unlike money in the bank, which we can count, we don't know how many years we have on this earth.

Give your time, but don't let people take it.

HOW TO TAKE ADVICE

One of the great lessons I learned, I learned from a pastor in California. Danny Silk teaches about honoring one another. That respect is vital in one of the most common interactions in relationships: the giving and taking of advice.

Everybody likes to share their opinion. Everyone wants to tell you what you should do. There's nothing wrong with having opinions, but there is something wrong with unsolicited advice, and it's rarely accepted.

Before giving an opinion, it's far better to ask for permission. Something as simple as, "Would you like to know what I think about that?" can open the door to a meaningful and helpful discussion. Without that permission, the response is almost always met with a closed mind and defensiveness.

Permission lowers the guard. When you give permission, you make yourself willing to receive what someone has to say because you value their opinion. And when you want to give advice, it gives you the opportunity to ask questions and give the other person the chance to discover so much about who they are. Often the answers we're looking for are there inside of us.

HOW TO SAY NO

Saying no can produce a backlash. If someone isn't healthy emotionally, they'll take it as an offense. That pushback creates a kind of parent/child relationship; one side says no, and the other tries to take what they want anyway. When you block them, they cry, throw a tantrum, or pitch a hissy fit because they're not getting their way. But we're not responsible for other people's hissy fits. We're responsible for loving others, and that doesn't always mean doing what they want us to do, even if they'll think less of us. That's not our responsibility. As Terry Cole-Whittaker put it, "What you think of me is none of my business."[3]

We can't worry about how others are going to react if we feel we are doing what is right for ourselves and for others.

Setting healthy boundaries also requires communicating your feelings. Others will either understand or they won't. They'll either apologize and change their behavior or, in the case of unhealthy codependency, they'll make excuses and not take your feelings into account.

Understanding is the goal of all communication. When we're communicating, we're trying to make the other person understand, whether it's something for the mind or something for the heart.

If you have somebody in your life who breaches your boundaries—and everyone does—you get to explain why you find their behavior unacceptable. You get to decide the consequences even if that means cutting them out of your life.

It's simple but it's not easy. Acting on those consequences

is hard. There's a big difference between responding and reacting. Reacting is emotional and responding is thoughtful. But as Henry Cloud and John Townsend understood, the result of not acting is even harder.

IT'S FUN TO SHARE YOUR FUN

"Man, you gotta try this!"

"You really should check out this movie."

"You have to read that book."

You gotta, you should, you have to . . . there's no shortage of people telling you what to do and how to do it. Sometimes you'll take their advice because you trust the people who are giving it to you. You try pogo-sticking or watch that Norwegian subtitled crime drama or read that book about initiation rites among the tribes of Pulau, and they leave you cold.

The person who gave you that recommendation was giving you bad information.

But they didn't mean to. They genuinely believed

you would enjoy the experience they were recommending. After all, they enjoyed it, so why wouldn't you?

There was another reason, though, that they were so enthusiastic about the advice they offered: it's fun to introduce people to things they'll love.

We all do it. We see a great movie, and we want to tell our friends. When they come out of the cinema with a big grin on their faces, we get to think: *Hey, I made that happen!* We meet a guy who would be perfect for a girl we know, and we look forward to the toast at the wedding. We fly twenty feet in the air attached to a piece of string, and we want to bring everyone with us.

Okay, we might not all want to do that, but that's what Ryan Steinolfson wanted to do. The owner of a marketing company, Ryan is also a water sports enthusiast—and like anyone who has found something that they enjoy, he wanted everyone to come along with him.

So when Ryan discovered the Periscope app that allows people to stream their live experiences, his first thought was, *Wow! You mean I can actually bring people along for the ride? In the moment?*

Ryan built a contraption that strapped a camera to the top of his head and told his social media audience that he was going kitesurfing. About two hundred people came with him as Ryan leapt off waves and hung in the air attached to a parachute before splashing back down into the water.

Ryan got to enjoy a double load of fun. He had a blast doing something he loved. And he doubled down on the fun knowing that he was showing lots of other people a really great time.

But something else happened while Ryan was enjoying himself. He was also building his business. Those live kitesurfing videos raised his online engagement levels by a factor of forty. People began to associate Ryan with high-adrenaline sporting activities. "They're like, 'When are we going to go kitesurfing again?'" he says.

Fun wants to be contagious. There's a pleasure in having it. There's also a pleasure—and a benefit—in sharing it. So while people "shoulding" on you isn't something you have to listen to, it is worth understanding that they're usually doing it for a good reason: they found something that's fun and they want you to have fun too.

⇥ 11 ⇤

HOORAY FOR FAILURE

Payal Kadakia just wanted to find a local dance class. A graduate of MIT, a consultant at Bain & Company, and a trained Indian and classical dancer, she was looking for a studio where she could continue to take dance classes in her spare time. An hour of googling and comparing later, she figured there had to be a better way to find a suitable studio. So in 2012 she launched Classtivity, a search engine for classes.

It didn't work.

The service was getting publicity. People would search for classes, but they weren't making bookings—and without the bookings, Classtivity wasn't making money. "I knew we had built an idea and a vision," she told *Inc.* magazine. "But we hadn't built a product that was working."

So Kadakia pivoted. She created a new product called Passport. For $49, users could take a single class at any participating studio in their area. That worked. The company had revenue. It even had profit. But the studio owners weren't happy. People would attend a class but not return. Kadakia's product had made it easier for them to give away free samples, but it wasn't helping their revenues.

Uncomfortable with the idea of building a business on the backs of dance and fitness studios, Kadakia pivoted again. This time she built a product called ClassPass which sold subscriptions. Users could take any class they wanted at any participating studio any number of times. One week they could bounce around in a Zumba class; the next, they could bend themselves into yoga shapes. Participation tripled month after month. After seeing the growth charts, one investor responded that Kadakia had created the next Uber.[1]

Success very rarely arrives immediately. It usually takes several attempts and several failures, but when you're working on something that's your passion, you keep going. You don't quit. It's only when you believe you can let your idea go and be okay that you know you're on the wrong track. When you're doing what you're supposed to be doing, there's always another way, another opportunity.

Understanding that you're on the right track, though, takes discernment, a skill that most of us don't come by naturally. When we're younger, our enthusiasm can carry us forward regardless, and we don't always see the signs that we're heading in the wrong direction. We always need to be asking ourselves: *Am I doing what I'm supposed to be doing? Is this in alignment with who I am and my passions and my talents, or did I get distracted by a bright, shiny object?*

When things go wrong—and they always go wrong—you have to ask whether it's fixable or whether there's something fundamentally wrong with the service or the product. Large companies set up focus groups to ask those questions; owners of small firms ask people they know and trust.

But just reaching a point where you're asking, "What's wrong here?" is a mark of success. It's proof that you're willing to try, knowing full well that your attempts could collapse. If you've enjoyed the process of experimentation, you've experienced success even if the product has failed.

FAIL SLOWLY

The usual advice regarding failure is to fail fast. If you're going to fail at something, get it over with quickly so you can move on to something else. But that's not always the case. Sometimes we need to fail slowly. My mobile marketing platform, described earlier, died gradually, and I needed to experience that slow death in order to fully appreciate the freedom of letting it go and moving on to something else. It was expensive, but I wouldn't have learned the lesson otherwise. What we learn and who we become in the process is more important than the success or failure of any one business.

It's the difference between earning wealth and inheriting it. If you haven't earned it, you don't appreciate it. But when you've taken your business down to the valley of the shadow

IF YOU'VE ENJOYED
THE PROCESS OF
EXPERIMENTATION,
YOU'VE EXPERIENCED
SUCCESS EVEN
IF THE PRODUCT
HAS FAILED.

of death, you value it. You know what failure looks like. You know what it feels and smells like. You know you don't want to go back there, and what you've learned from spending your time there is going to help, hopefully, to ensure that it won't happen again. Never again will I put several years into a business that's just not working. Failure is always the price you pay for a valuable lesson.

It's also what makes aiming high so rewarding. You might miss spectacularly, but even if you come away empty-handed, you'll be walking away with valuable knowledge that you can take and apply to new businesses.

Except that sometimes you can't, at least not directly. Sometimes your next project is so different from the previous one that it's hard to apply the lessons of a failure and even harder to duplicate a success. I had a huge success with the iFart app. We generated two million downloads and hit the number-one spot in the iTunes App Store for a three-week period. But I never had another app success that big. Sometimes you just run into the perfect storm: the right time, the right place, the right product, the right messaging, the right media outlets, the right celebrity using it. You never know what's going to launch you into the stratosphere.

Nor do you know how many times you'll need to jump on that springboard. The reality is that a period of success doesn't guarantee ongoing success. After ClassPass took off, Kadakia's app started to run into trouble. Offering unlimited subscriptions allowed users to take classes daily, in effect for just a few dollars at a time. Studio chains started to pull out. Kadakia had to push up prices. A monthly $99 for users in

New York City shot up to $199, causing some users to cancel their subscriptions. Kadakia has since resigned as CEO, though she has remained as chairman of the company.[2] Finding a dance class where Kadakia could indulge her passion might have taken a frustrating hour, but indulging her passion in business might well give her a lifetime of enjoyable challenges.

Succeeding at a project is an incredibly rewarding feeling. But the lessons learned while in the valley, whether personally or professionally, are the impetus for unprecedented growth. Don't be afraid of failure. Instead see it as one of your greatest mentors. It's all part of the process.

⇥12⇤

BE WILLING TO SHIFT

We have a habit of asking children the hardest question in the world. We ask them: "What are you going to be when you grow up?" That question is intended to elicit a categorical response, but a wisecracking kid is likely to say: "I'm going to be me."

There's actually a great deal of wisdom in this response, because that's really all we can ever be: a human being consisting of all the unique characteristics that make us who we are.

Even if the questioner, after rolling their eyes, changes the question to: "What are you going to *do* when you grow up?" the answer shouldn't be much better. I've done more things than I can count since I started making pizzas and slinging submarine sandwiches at age fourteen. I've been a health club janitor; a clerk at a toy store, a video store, and a department store; a DJ at a nightclub; a radio DJ; an encyclopedia salesman; a radio program editor; and a data entry manager, and that was all before my internet entrepreneurial journey even began. Since then, I've done everything online that's not illegal, immoral, or fattening: building sites, selling sites, domain name brokering, eBay selling, creating and selling information products, internet marketing, affiliate marketing, social media marketing, video creation, live video, blogging, podcasting, writing books, public speaking, and more.

There's no one thing that defines you. Life is full of opportunities to pivot to new ideas. You don't have to take those opportunities if you don't want to. For me, variety allows me to stay engaged and have fun, but that might not be for everybody. Other people are content to do one thing for that season of their life. But part of having fun is the spontaneous shifting that occurs when you least expect it, when the opportunity arises and you decide that you want to just go and play with it. Even for those whose working lives follow a straighter line— doctors, teachers, lawyers—the happiest are often those who can find some diversity in what they do or who have active interests outside their clinics, classrooms, and offices.

Some of those things that people love to do in their free time might even make money on the side. They might even make more selling on eBay or photographing the occasional wedding than they earn in their day job, but they love treating people, teaching kids, and helping people in legal trouble. In the end, it's not about how much you earn, but what you love to do that defines you.

ASK FOR A BETTER LIFE—OR BUILD ONE!

One of the reasons that people look outside their day jobs for a creative, satisfying outlet is that they're often allowed so little creativity in their workplace. Back when I was young and employed (shudder . . .), I was often fired from jobs for suggesting new ways of doing things. My bosses found it threatening. They had been doing things a certain way for a long time, and they didn't want to change. They certainly didn't want somebody who could take their job, push them out, skip over them, and land the promotion that they thought they deserved.

But not every workplace is like that. Sometimes you just need to ask for the freedom to be more creative in your work. Asking is often the simplest and most powerful way to get what you want. Whether you want a promotion, a raise, greater responsibility, or even if you're just not happy with the food that's been served to you in a restaurant and want to try something different, there's one truth I discovered that I repeatedly told my kids as they were growing up: it never hurts to ask. My kids used to roll their eyes at this, but I have a feeling this teaching has become useful to them now that they're young adults.

What's the worst thing that can happen when you ask? They can only say no. I have received so many great gifts from others either in terms of goods or services, just by asking.

**ASKING IS OFTEN
THE SIMPLEST AND
MOST POWERFUL
WAY TO GET WHAT
YOU WANT.**

It helps to ask carefully. French-American industrial designer Raymond Loewy coined the term MAYA, an acronym for "Most Advanced, Yet Acceptable." His argument was that the process of change can be slow, so if you want to push a new idea, you need to link it with something old. People are more comfortable with evolution than revolution.

There's very little that's really new under the sun. Pivots usually just shift direction and use the momentum of a current movement rather than attempting 180-degree turns. All knowledge and wisdom is fully available; we just put a little twist on it.

Even if you're careful, though, asking will produce rejection. But rejection isn't a rejection of you as a person unless you take it that way. It's a rejection of *that idea*. And ideas are easy. Most should be rejected.

REJECTION AND THE POWER OF SELF-REJECTION

James Altucher is a hedge fund manager, entrepreneur, and podcaster. Every day, without fail, he writes down ten ideas. That's ten ideas every day from someone who has twice sold a company he founded for $10 million and now writes a column for *The Financial Times*.

How many of those ideas does he act on and turn into something valuable? It's unlikely to be more than one or two a year because ideas are a dime a dozen. They come when you're out walking, listening to podcasts, or in the shower. (There's something about the shower in particular that's effective for me. I think it creates a meditative state that allows the mind to do its thing!)

Few of the ideas I have every day become more than a thought. Some of them make it to a "consider" list. A few make it to a to-do list. Only a very small percentage ever come to fruition, because you have to toss out a lot of ideas to find the gem. It's like looking for a diamond at the bottom of a mine. It's rare. It's hard to find. But you know it when you see it.

You'll still have to dig it out and polish it and test it to find out if it's real. Before I act on any idea, I'll take it to a friend, someone knowledgeable and smart, and invite him to whack it as hard as he can and try to break it apart. Only a friend will be that honest. Only a friend will tell you when your face is dirty. They might try to save your feelings, but they know they don't need to.

When I was working for Hope for the Heart radio in Dallas, I heard June Hunt, the station's chief service officer, talk about delivering criticism like a sandwich. You always start with the bread of encouragement, add the meat of criticism, then wrap it up with another slice of encouragement so that people don't feel as if you're just beating up on them. Not everyone can do that, which is why only a small group of people ever know what I'm working on. The rest won't know until the launch.

When I show my plan to that friend or that small group, I'll usually walk away thinking, *What a stupid idea I had!* But sometimes, the idea survives. The criticism doesn't scratch the surface, and I'll know I've got something real and shiny.

And then the work begins, because in the end, only execution is worth something. If you can pull it off and make it profitable, then you've got something—and that's hard. I've seen eight-figure deals negotiated and planned only to crumble overnight. Nothing is ever anything until it's something, and a lot of people fall in love with the idea rather than loving the process. The process matters.

But if you have a good idea and it's rejected, and you really want to make it happen—if you feel that your creativity is being stifled and squashed—that's when you have to move. You have to decide whether there is something you could do in your off hours to find your creative escape, or you need to look for something completely different. Even if you need to provide for your family and you're in a season of life in which you need to make sacrifices, you can at least begin dreaming about an escape route. Once your dream is ready, you can start believing that there's a way to actually make it happen.

It's always worth remembering, though, that there are no limits on entrepreneurs. When you have your own business, you get to decide. You make the rules. That's why I can find an idea that really interests me, turn on a dime, and test it to see if it will work, regardless of the risk.

DON'T FEAR THE PIRATES

One problem with pushing out new ideas is that they can be copied. Within a month or two of iFart being a hit, the App Store had about two hundred copycat apps! (None of the others really made much of a dent. Turns out there's only so much room for digital flatulence on your smartphone.) My e-books are regularly stolen. I used to try get them taken down whenever I'd get a Google alert that one of my books had appeared on some Russian download site, but I don't sweat it anymore. Now my attitude is, if they need it bad enough to steal it, then they can have it.

And copying can be good for business. Neil Gaiman found that when people in Russia would translate his books and put them on download sites, his sales in that country would go up. People discovered him. He even persuaded his publisher to put *American Gods*, which has since been made into a television series, online for free for a month. Sales in independent bookstores, the only place the publisher measured, increased by 300 percent.[1] The Grateful Dead became one of the most financially successful rock bands in the world by encouraging people to record and share their concerts.

Push out an idea and sure, someone might steal it. But if people know that the original came from you, you'll benefit and you'll find yourself moving in the direction you want to go.

If there's one thing we can be absolutely certain of in this world, it's that there is no certainty. We live in a dynamic world, and change is truly the only constant. Knowing this can help you prepare for change and not be caught off guard. A prepared mind is less likely to react and more likely to thoughtfully respond.

If you are publishing copyrighted material, it will likely be stolen.

If you put forth an idea, someone will reject it.

And if you think that the way things are is the way things will always be, you are in for a rude awakening.

Shift happens. Expect it and you will be better prepared to go with the flow. This mind-set will lead to a happier, healthier you. And yes, you'll have more FUN!

FUN IS A GAME, NOT A CONTEST

Hockey players aren't known for their caring, compassionate nature. They're better known for squashing rival players against the wall for daring to look at their puck the wrong way. But that's not how Kim Garst likes to play. After months of taking her kids to hockey practice and waiting for the game to end, she and the other hockey moms decided to get together and form their own women's hockey league.

For Kim, that was the easy part. The tough part was ignoring the shouts from her husband to stop helping rival players back on to their feet after they'd been knocked down on the ice.

Kim is the CEO and cofounder of Boom! Social,

a digital and social media marketing firm in Tampa, Florida. Her job is to help people, so it was natural for her to stop on the ice and help whenever she saw someone down and out. It's what she does all day, whether she's talking to her million-plus community members or setting a strategy for a corporate client. The fun of her job is lifting other people up.

But no one is up all the time. Everyone faces challenges in their business or setbacks in their career. Everyone has moments when it feels like they're sitting on the ice and the other players are flying right past them. And not everyone has someone like Kim Garst prepared to stop and extend them a hand.

At times like those, even an activity you love can feel a long way from fun. However much you might like playing in a baseball league or creating marketing campaigns, they can both feel pretty unpleasant if you keep swinging and missing or if your campaigns keep failing. It takes time to learn to do anything well, but when the learning process feels like it's taking forever, it can be tempting to believe that you're heading in the wrong direction and need to point yourself toward a different goal.

That's especially true when you see other people moving much faster than you toward the destination that you want to reach.

But life isn't a game and it's not a contest. There are no medals for getting there before someone else, and there's no place in the Guinness World Records for the fastest-built business or the most new clients collected in one year.

"The only competition we're in is with ourselves," says Kim Garst. "I'm not trying to compete. I'm just trying to complete my own race."

Business is a competitive environment. You'll always be battling other people for the same dollars, whether you're applying for a new position or trying to land a new customer. But there's also plenty of room for everyone at the end of the journey. Just as the fun in a game of hockey is the time you spend on the ice, not the score on the board at the end of the game, so there's always more fun in a business's activities than in its size or value.

Competition is a good thing, but win today or win tomorrow, the key is to enjoy the game.

⇒13⇐

THE IMPORTANCE OF
SHOWING UP

Back in 2006 I was invited to attend Yanik Silver's Underground Online Marketing Seminar in Washington, DC. One of the more popular events at the time, Silver's seminar attracted an audience of information marketers who were quietly making serious bank online while working at home in shorts and T-shirts.

While I was there, a young guy with long, blond hair walked up to me. He looked like a cross between a hippy and a Viking. He introduced himself as Eric Holmlund and handed me a flier announcing that he was seeking joint venture projects. It said simply, "JV with Eric."

In the internet marketing and affiliate marketing space, the term *joint venture* is often misused. When someone says, "JV with me," he or she usually just means "promote my stuff." A true joint venture is a partnership of sorts where two people and/or businesses create, develop, and launch a product together. I discovered that this is the kind of joint venture Eric was seeking. Smart.

We talked and I just took to him right away. We shared some values, had a similar sense of humor, and he told me that he was familiar with the book I'd recently published teaching people how to make money with Google AdSense.

"If there was ever a way that we could find something to do together, and it would be profitable and helpful for people, we should investigate it," he said. I didn't have anything in mind at the time, but I told him that if he had any ideas to let me know.

A couple weeks later, he sent me a message. "I have a great idea," he said. "Your AdSense teachings, both your e-book and your physical book, are helping thousands of people understand how to make money with their website, but most of them are struggling just to get websites up and running. What if we created a product that provided a template for websites with a variety of different headers for different niches? We'd teach them how to create content, and all they'd have to do to build a website quickly and easily is insert their AdSense code."

It made perfect sense to me. Before the launch of Wordpress, the most popular site-building tool today, there wasn't an easy way to do what Eric proposed. So we produced a product called Instant AdSense Templates and launched it in the summer of that year. Customers gladly paid $197, and the product grossed more than $300,000.

Because it was so successful, we revisited what worked and what didn't and came up with Instant AdSense Templates 2, a more advanced and comprehensive solution. AdSense was huge at this time and the opportunity was ripe. We priced the product (shipped on CD-ROM at the time) at $197 with a $97 upsell and a membership subscription. We understood that scarcity and urgency were legitimate, effective tools for making sales, so we limited the product launch to seven days with a million-dollar sales cap. The product sold out in five days. We made a lot of money and our affiliates made a lot of money.

Shortly after the success of this launch, Eric and I began wondering what we might do next. The reality show *The Apprentice* had recently become a massive hit, and around the same time I became interested in online video and began posting on YouTube.

One day while in the shower (I told you I get so many ideas there!), I pondered a merging of the two. I wondered what would happen if we combined an idea for a reality show with the rise of YouTube. I talked about it with Eric, and we came up with an idea for a broadcast-quality, reality television show about internet marketing that would be distributed online.

It was hugely ambitious. *The Next Internet Millionaire* was a thirteen-episode reality show. We auditioned hundreds of contestants, created a set, brought in high-profile internet marketing teachers, filmed with four hi-definition cameras, edited each episode to fifty minutes, and produced a real show with a real prize. I was the executive producer and the host, and Eric was the producer and director. Somehow we pulled it off. The show received an honorary Webby Award and has its own *Wikipedia* page.

The entire process was super fun, and it all came from one meeting at one event where I took a few minutes to chat with a long-haired young fellow.

GET THEE TO AN EVENT

The moral of that story is you never know what's going to happen when you put yourself out there. Social media is great and the internet is a fantastic way to communicate, but we have to show up, shake hands, and meet people face-to-face. That's why when people ask me the best way to get started with their business, I don't tell them which book to read or site to register or online tool to buy. I tell them to find an event in their area of interest and go. Even if they don't know anybody, they should go. Even if they're an introvert, they should go. Social Media Marketing World, for example, is the biggest social media marketing event on the calendar, and one of the first sessions teaches introverts how to network, feel welcome, and make contacts.

The information presented at these events is important, but you'll encounter some of the most valuable content at any event in the hallways. When I go to events, I rarely sit still to hear somebody speak. That's partly because I can't sit still for very long. I've got a lot of energy, and when I'm at an event

YOU NEVER KNOW
WHAT'S GOING TO
HAPPEN WHEN
YOU PUT YOURSELF
OUT THERE.

and have so many people around me that I know and so many new people that I haven't met yet, I find it hard to sit still for an hour. I'm also worried I might learn something.

Irony alert!

Now, don't get me wrong, there's nothing wrong with learning. I hope you are learning some valuable things from this book. But the truth is, at these events I have picked up so much knowledge that I haven't implemented that I often end up "shoulding" on myself, worrying that I'm not using that list-building technique or that graphic tactic. I end up frustrated with myself about the things I am *not* doing. So while learning is great, I approach events not mainly as information-gathering opportunities but as people-meeting opportunities. I've discovered that relationships forged and discussions in the hallway are infinitely more valuable to me than whatever I learn in seminars, because I can take what I already have and try to help someone or explore ways for us to work together.

And sometimes I just get to meet some great people, which is a pleasure in itself. I had heard of an entrepreneur and professional speaker named Mitch Joel. But once we connected at a live event, I befriended Mitch and discovered a kindred spirit who shares a similar philosophy of fun. Mitch runs a very successful digital marketing agency. He employs more than 2,200 people in 45 different countries, gives talks, and writes books. But with fun and quality of life at the forefront of his priorities, Mitch still makes time to produce a popular podcast about bass guitarists. He gets to meet his heroes and talk about a topic they both love. I wouldn't have met Mitch, discovered these wonderful passions of his, and made a new friend if I hadn't gone to that particular event. There are always rewards for just getting out there and talking to people.

THE VALUE OF A CONVERSATION

The events you attend don't have to be as large as Social Media Marketing World. People in a variety of markets put on small, intimate events, sometimes with as few as ten people. I've seen relationships come out of those events that are just as powerful as anything that's happened at a five-thousand-person event. In fact, the more intimate the event, the more everybody there gets to know what everybody else does. They're more likely to make a real connection that persists beyond the event.

A few years ago, I organized a book event with David Hancock, the publisher of my AdSense book. We had around thirty people come for a one-day book camp. We taught them everything we knew about the publishing industry and book marketing. We got to know all the people in the room, and we're now seeing their books coming out. It's really rewarding because we know we poured directly into a small group and it was effective.

Lots of people can say that they were part of an event with thousands of people, but attending an event with a small group feels special. There's power in that. Deeper can be stronger than bigger. I encourage people to attend local meetup groups to deliver big results. You'll meet someone, and now you've got a new friend or a business possibility. It's like fishing: you cast your line, and often when you pull it back there's nothing on the hook. But sometimes you catch a big one. (I think this is true, but since I dislike fishing, I don't know for sure.) If you don't know where to start, go online, look at the calendar of what's happening nearby, find something that has a connection to you even if it's not directly related to business, and put yourself out there. You may be surprised how this small effort can bring big results. That's working smart, and it's fun!

DOING THE REAL WORK

People often say they're starting a new business when what they really mean is they're building a website or designing a business card or hiring someone to make them a logo. But that's not what matters the most in creating a new venture. The real work is going out, meeting people, getting customers, and getting your ideas out there, even if nothing sticks for a while. One thing I learned in my early days of sales was SW, SW, SW—or SW^3: Some Will, Some Won't, So What?

The more people you talk to, the greater the chances that you will create a fun new opportunity, because you never know what will stick, either for the person you meet or for yourself. One result of that networking is a rediscovery of yourself. Usually as children and into early adulthood, we start discovering what we like and what we don't like, but knowing yourself is a lifelong process. We go through seasons of change and need to regularly examine ourselves to discover who we are and where we are in any given season of life. It's why people talk about going away to find themselves. We all need that time. We're always learning more so that as we discover perhaps an innate talent or a proclivity toward a particular area, we can explore it.

For example, I'd never taken a Master Class. I'm not going to learn how to cook with Gordon Ramsay, and while learning to act with Dustin Hoffman might be fun, the only role I can play well is my own. But one day an ad on my Facebook feed offered me Steve Martin and his comedy Master Class.

Now, I grew up watching Steve Martin. I can remember the first time he was on *Saturday Night Live*, playing his banjo, when his hair was still dark. The ad had me at "Hi, my name is Steve." I clicked that buy button faster than you could say, "Well excuussssse meeeee!"

And while I have spoken in front of thousands of people, I've never done a stand-up routine before. It sounded fun . . . and terrifying! It opened up this piece of me that I hadn't explored before. It's now on my bucket list to do a stand-up routine. Perhaps I'll end up being more of a sit-down comic, or a sit-down-and-shut-up comic (buh-dum-bum), but I just know I want to try it. I might only do a few minutes and the response might be crickets. I don't know whether it will improve my talks or have no effect on them at all. I don't know if I would have thought of it if I hadn't seen that ad in my Facebook stream. But it sounded like fun, and I'm also aware that some of those things we try as hobbies can end up becoming monetizable.

This is why it's also important not to allow our identities

to get wrapped up in what we do. That old saying "We are human beings, not human doings" works. If we're getting our love, our significance, and our belonging from our behavior, then we're looking in the wrong place because it can change in a moment. Our identity is not found in our country of origin. It's not in our names, and it's not in our activities.

What do people who take their careers and make it their identity do when they lose that career? What do people who find their identity in their relationships with others do when those relationships end? We have to know ourselves as deeply as possible. We have to enter a lifelong journey of exploration, and the paths of that exploration run through meeting people, talking with them, and being open to the opportunities that those relationships offer. It's a most enjoyable way to explore who you really are.

A journalist once asked British Prime Minister Harold Macmillan what the leader of a government fears the most. "Events, dear boy, events," he said. But events are nothing to be afraid of. They're where the biggest opportunities are found.

⇒14⇐

THE HUSTLE IS A DANCE AND GRINDING IS FOR COFFEE BEANS

One Friday evening I was having dinner at a casual restaurant with a small group of friends—the kind of guys who have goals, work hard, and have plenty of drive. The waitress came over and, as she pulled out her pad, said: "So do you guys have exciting plans for the weekend?"

Straight away three of my friends replied: "Oh, we're just going to hustle and grind."

They said those words without a thought. The hustle and grind is expected. It's fashionable. It's cool. And it makes me cringe.

Each of those friends has his own skills and his own talents. One can aim a marketing campaign like Robin Hood with a telescopic sight, while another is always coming up with great product ideas. It's those skills, and the passion they feel when they use them, that will determine whether or not they reach their goals. It won't be the hustle and grind they put in, because there is no guarantee that a certain number of hours worked and a certain amount of sacrifice made will get the results you want. Plenty of people have hustled and ground their lives away and never received the reward that they thought they deserved. We hear about the people who succeeded but rarely the ones who fell by the wayside.

That sounds tragic, but heading off the road of hustle and grind might actually be the path you want to take. The things we say we want aren't always what we actually want, and what we want the most we often undervalue.

NOTHING TEACHES YOU LIKE LIFE

One of life's challenges is that wisdom comes through experience. Yes, it can be imparted to some degree—we can tell the next generation the things they should know, and they could heed that wisdom—but nothing teaches you like life. There's no lesson more powerful than touching the hot stove and feeling the burn.

That isn't to say that young people can't have their heads screwed on right. Some understand what they're going after and follow their passion. They're not driven by money, so when they reach their destination they don't feel lost.

In 2011, Yalda T. Uhls and Patricia Greenfield published a study they had conducted at the UCLA campus of the Children's Digital Media Center, Los Angeles. What they found was that around 2007—about the same time that *Keeping Up with the Kardashians* and reality TV became a phenomenon—children's values changed.

In previous years, asked to rank sixteen values by priority, preteens had put "community feeling" as their first or second choice. Now, membership of a group was ranked eleventh and top of the list was "fame." One eleven-year-old boy told the researchers, "My friends and I are making a YouTube channel. . . . Our goal is to try and get a million subscribers."[1]

Other surveys have shown similar results. Children consistently put being known above acquiring the skill and knowledge that they might be known for—and they might well succeed. Mark Schaefer is a marketing strategist and the author of *Known*, a guide to personal branding. He wanted to know whether anyone could make themselves famous. He examined whether there was a process that anyone could use to reach the goal that those kids now most wanted: to become known.

After interviewing a hundred people in fields ranging from banking and education to real estate and construction, Schaefer found that there was indeed a system, and it worked for everyone.[2] Anyone has the opportunity now to be famous—if that's what they want. But when they get it, they may well find they don't want it. When Tom Cruise was married to Nicole

Kidman, she said they could only tour Rome at night; they'd be mobbed if they tried to do it during the day.

For adults, the wealth and the power brought by fame might look more attractive than fame itself, but they, too, have their costs. They bring new responsibilities, demands, and dangers. It's very easy to expand the cost of living to match earnings, to buy a bigger house, a boat, a vacation home. And then if the money stops, you go bankrupt. The fall is harder than the rise. Wealth and power are the unstated goals of a hustle and grind lifestyle, and none of it is ultimately satisfying. What *is* satisfying is trying to change the world, trying to make it a better place. Everything else is an overvalued forgery.

HUSTLING AND HEALTH

The only time the hustle is good for your health is if you are doing the dance of the same name from the midseventies. Other than that, you can hustle and grind your way to an early grave. If you're not paying attention to your health, then that work will just kill you.

After I sold my company to Yahoo, I took time to work on my physical being. I was about fifty pounds overweight, taking medication for high-blood pressure, and the doctor wasn't too happy about my cholesterol either. My hours and hours of work didn't help because most of that work was sedentary, sitting in front of my computer.

So I made a decision. I decided it was time to become healthier.

WEALTH AND POWER ARE THE UNSTATED GOALS OF A HUSTLE AND GRIND LIFESTYLE, AND NONE OF IT IS ULTIMATELY SATISFYING.

Notice that I didn't say I would *try* to become healthier. I said I made a decision to do it.

This is actually essential and reveals the reason that many people who *try* to do something ultimately fail. It's because trying to do something leaves you a way out. It signals that you doubt your own ability to do it. It sets you up to fail.

It's the reason most New Year's resolutions fail after that first visit to the health club. You haven't really decided to do this thing you say you want to do, at least not enough to truly commit.

That great green sage Yoda summed it up perfectly: "Do. Or do not. There is no try."

My decision to lose weight and become more fit was a done deal from the moment I decided. In my mind, I was that man who fit into size 34 jeans and no longer needed any medication. Everything else was just the process taking place. (See how that concept of process is recurring?)

Over the next five months, I made choices that were commensurate with the decision I had made. And while I am no doctor, nutritionist, or fitness guru, I can share with you a simple plan that will help you lose weight and become more fit. Be sure to highlight this because it will change your life.

Eat less and move your body more.

I'm not suggesting you starve yourself, but let's face it, our Western world food portions are ridiculous. We stuff ourselves. And we eat too much sugar and fried food.

Combine that with our more sedentary, consumer lifestyle, and is it any wonder that obesity and diabetes are at an all-time high?

My decision was simple. Cut back on portions and stop eating fried foods and desserts on a regular basis. Add to that an hour or so of walking every day. Fresh air and sunshine provided amazing results for me. It's one of the reasons I live in Denver, Colorado, with more than three hundred days of sunshine each year. Not only is fresh air and moving your body good for you physically, but the mental benefits are superb. I use that time to listen to podcasts, soak up teaching, catch up with friends or family, or enjoy music. All the while, my brain is at work and I come up with some fantastic ideas.

The simple decision to eat less and move my body more brought satisfying results quite naturally, all without hustling and grinding away at the gym.

There's nothing wrong with selecting a healthy nutritional diet. Nor is there a problem with going to the gym and pumping iron if that's what you want to do. But just because culture is leaning toward the Donut Diet (oh, were that a thing!) or the Macarena Fitness Plan (and I'm glad that's not), doesn't mean it's right for you.

I found what worked for me, and it wasn't complicated.

You might think that changing your diet or implementing an exercise plan wouldn't be fun, but once I had made the decision to do so, it actually did become fun. I think it's because I was doing what I wanted to do and I knew I would celebrate the results.

While losing weight and getting fit help you to feel better and become more productive, there is another medicine that goes directly to the idea of fun, and it doesn't require a prescription.

Laughter.

According to a 2009 paper by William B. Strean, a number of clinical trials have validated the therapeutic efficacy of laughter in medical fields including geriatrics, oncology, critical care, psychiatry, rehabilitation, rheumatology, home care, palliative care, hospice care, and general patient care.[3] It's not something you'd want to rely on. If you're in the emergency ward with a broken arm and the doctor tells you that he can either give you a cast or tell you a joke, take the cast. But laughter helps, so in addition to finding time for that walk, take the time to do something that makes you grin. It doesn't have to be Laughter Yoga; your favorite comedy show can do the trick. The internet is rife with funny videos that your friends are all too eager to share with you. If I'm desperate for a laugh, I just think of some of the silly things I've done, and that provides some of the best material.

If you're laughing, it can't be bad. If you're smiling, you're in the moment and enjoying the good feelings. It's certainly better than using the money you gained from hustle and grind to pay medical bills caused by overwork.

WE ARE THREE-PART BEINGS

Finally, the hustle and grind isn't good for spiritual health either. Man is a three-part being. We are physical; we have our body, which is our mobile home on this earth. We are emotional, which is our mind, will, and emotions. And we're spiritual. At least I believe we are. It's that part of us that is a spark of the Divine, that is made to live eternally. I believe the three are designed to work together toward the healthiest you you can be.

The best way to take care of all three of those parts is to lead a life with meaning, and it's never too late to start. As long as you have a pulse, you have time. There are plenty of stories of people who didn't start to reach their goals until later in life. Martha Stewart didn't publish her first book until she was forty-one. Vera Wang only became a designer at forty. Ray Kroc was over fifty when he bought his first McDonald's. Colonel Harland David Sanders didn't start selling his Kentucky Fried Chicken until he was sixty-five. Shall I go on?

It starts with fun. It starts with that mind-set shift, with abandoning old ideas that you've discovered haven't worked or are past their sell-by date. And it's hard to change. Ideas and beliefs die hard, whether they're religious beliefs or ideas about money or notions about the people in our lives. When we discover that what we thought was true is actually false, it can be a real swipe at our identity. We either go into defensive mode or we allow those beliefs to crumble around us and take the consequences.

You might find that you don't want that big house, and if you sold it and moved ten miles outside of the city, you could be happier. If you quit that job and did something else, you could still make it. But nothing happens until you do something. You have to take action.

It's okay to take risks, if those risks move you forward. It's okay to change your mind, if you find you were wrong or if the situation changes. I change my mind so regularly that

I've become used to not planning too far ahead so that I have space to live today and to take advantage if the right opportunities, the right people, the right place, or the right things present themselves.

But those things can take time, and few of us are good at waiting. The only way to get patience is to exercise it. It starts as kids when everything seems like an eternity away. The summer break never comes, and then it feels like it will never end. We count down to Christmas and birthdays and trips to Disney World and then we become adults and we shed that anticipation. We come to understand that it happens when it happens. We discover that the efforts we make to try to hurry the process lead to frustration, that hustling and grinding to get there now doesn't allow for personal growth. It doesn't allow opportunities to open in their own time.

That doesn't mean that we don't move forward in pursuit of that which is important to us.

NOT TAKING NO FOR AN ANSWER

In 2010 I released a book called *KaChing: How to Run an Online Business that Pays and Pays*. It demonstrated how anyone could monetize content online with advertising, information products, member sites, and so on. To promote the book, I borrowed inspiration from Staples and its "that was easy" button, manufacturing a button of my own. This one was green and sported a dollar sign on top. It doesn't take much imagination to know what kind of sound the button made when pressed.

I thought the KaChing Button would make for a fun novelty app. Tap the button on your device, and the hills are alive with the sound of money! So my team developed the app, and we submitted it to the App Store.

Imagine my surprise when the app was rejected by Apple for having "minimal user functionality." A cursory glance at the App Store revealed literally hundreds of apps that did just one thing.

When we hit these kinds of brick walls in business, it's easy just to give up and move on. I choose to take the approach of making lemonade with the lemons I'm handed.

I downloaded a number of apps that did very little and shot a short video poking fun at them, directing it to Steve Jobs in the form of an appeal. Since others in the tech space were puzzled by the lack of transparency in the App Store, the video got distributed and written about on multiple blogs. I then updated the app so that you could select one of four currency symbols to display on top of the button. It was approved a week later!

Just because someone tells you no doesn't mean that it's all over. And the answer isn't simply more hustle and grind. A simple and humorous approach that didn't involve working hard turned out to be very effective for KaChing. Are you seeing a pattern here? It's woven throughout the fabric of this book. But this isn't a pattern you superimpose on your life. Rather, you superimpose your life on the pattern, creating your own unique footprint that is likely to maximize your effectiveness—and your fun!

LIVE THE LIFE YOU'RE MOST CAPABLE OF LIVING

When John Lee Dumas completed eight years of service as an officer in the Army, he was ready for something different. Those eight years had included thirteen months in Iraq, leading a squad of sixteen men in territory as challenging as Fallujah. It was hard. It was also dangerous. A quarter of the men in John's platoon didn't return.

At each funeral, John committed to honoring those heroes by promising to live the life only he was fully capable of living.

Like many people, though, John struggled to find that calling.

His first stop was law school. He lasted a semester.

In Boston he joined the offices of John Hancock, an investment firm, and did a little better. He lasted eighteen months. A start-up in New York City introduced him to the fun of the Big Apple, but the job wasn't enjoyable enough to hold him there. He drove across country and took a job in real estate in San Diego, determined this time to see it through.

It wasn't long before he was regretting his choice. The real estate market had just tanked, and the work soon became routine.

"It was a grind," he recalls. "It was waking up in the morning. It was commuting into work. It was sitting in a cubicle. It was nose to the grindstone for eight or nine hours, commuting home, then going to bed so that I could do it all over again."

It certainly wasn't living the life he was fully capable of living.

But that commute gave John the inspiration he was looking for. As he sat in his car in San Diego traffic, he started listening to podcasts. He started with NPR but soon found himself listening to entrepreneur leaders such as Pat Flynn and Jaime Masters. And he started to wonder why no one was creating a daily podcast that featured interviews with leading entrepreneurs. Commuters like him would be able to listen each morning and arrive at the office with an understanding of their biggest mistakes, their greatest "aha" moments, and what they did to build success.

If no one else was doing it, John decided, he would.

Entrepreneur on Fire launched in September 2012 and soon built up a community of followers. He followed the advice his interviewees gave him, launching successful Kickstarter campaigns to create products that could help other entrepreneurs.

It wasn't long before John had left San Diego and was no longer working in real estate. He now lives in a house in Puerto Rico overlooking the Caribbean where he builds his podcast business full-time.

He also no longer has to grind, nor does he want to. Smart scheduling gives him bursts of intense focus lasting around half an hour before he takes a walk in the Caribbean sun or just takes time to refresh.

There's a time and a place for the hustle. There is a season for all things. But hustling all the time leads to burnout. When you do the things that really interest you, that's when you have the greatest outcomes. It's what I call trusting the process.

John Lee has learned to trust the process and discovered that he's living the life he loves.

⇾15⇽

A LITTLE LEVERAGE
GOES A LONG WAY

When we try to do everything ourselves, two things can happen: we eventually burn out, or we just don't do the job well. We do much better when we bring people with similar goals but different gifts, talents, and abilities to the table. As I look through my own projects, I can see that I try to do as little of the execution on a project as possible. I come up with the idea. I set the entrepreneurial vision. I lead. I do some marketing. Design? No. Copywriting? Not my favorite thing to do. Programming? I can't code my way out of a paper bag. Other technical stuff? I can dabble in some of the basics, but there are plenty of people who will do it much better and enjoy it more. Administrative tasks? Ugh, just shoot me now.

The real key to getting things done is summed up in one word: *leverage*. As I examine my track record, I realize this is something I've always done intuitively. Call it lazy or call it smart, but either way I look for people who can supply the strengths I lack, and I partner with them to get more done with less effort.

That's not something that people want to talk about. Everyone likes to boast about how they sweat over a project or how many hours they worked this week. No one likes to talk about how they managed to get a bunch of other people together to make a project fly. Again, it goes back to this odd mentality that long hours deserve applause. "Atta-boy, you worked an eighty-hour week!" I'd much rather say I worked four hours (with a nod to Tim Ferriss) and accomplished similar results.

Times have changed. Previous generations might have had a need for longer hours. If you weren't at the factory or on the farm, crops weren't growing and things weren't being produced, and you weren't earning. Those are the stories we've heard from our parents and grandparents, and they've been passed down through the generations. But we live in a different time. We can produce much faster and more efficiently than we ever could before. During the 2016 election campaign, there was a lot of talk about the declining coal industry. At the end of the Second World War, America had nearly half a million coal miners. Today, it has about a tenth of that number, but those fifty thousand miners produce almost twice as much coal as their grandparents did because they have better machines. They still work hard, but they also work smarter.

The constant sweat that once served us well and helped us prosper is no longer a key to success. More hours no longer lead to more output. Leveraging allows you to find people with whom you've already established a relationship, or can forge a mutually beneficial relationship, to explore an opportunity. Leveraging is about examining your most important current assets: the people in your life.

LEVERAGING IS NOT NETWORK MARKETING

There is a difference between leveraging relationships in a healthy way and using people. I know this will offend some people, but it's one of the reasons I'm not a fan of network marketing. While some companies (and individuals) have grown beyond this mentality, a chief strategy of network marketing companies has been to encourage people to go after their warm market first. They recommend recruiting family, friends, and associates to be in their downline. They don't just turn relationships into assets, they turn them into assets that deliver more rewards in one direction than they do in the other.

That's not what relationships are for, and it's not what leveraging is about. Sometimes multilevel marketing and network marketing put some people above others. The rewards

THE CONSTANT
SWEAT THAT ONCE
SERVED US WELL
AND HELPED US
TO PROSPER IS
NO LONGER A KEY
TO SUCCESS.

vary with your place in a vertical structure. Leveraging is different. It's more like a hub and spoke: one person connects everyone together, but everyone then rolls as one, taking the strain together and arriving together.

One way to think of it is as a more commercial version of crowdfunding. Anyone trying to raise funds for a business idea on Kickstarter needs help. First, they need help to create the campaign: to write the copy, shoot the video, and build the prototype. There are companies that now specialize in creating crowdfunding campaigns, but they're expensive. If you ask friends to help, it's likely they'll lend a hand because they want to see you succeed. If you then work your networks to alert people and persuade their friends to contribute, they'll do that, too, for the same reason. But if you offer them a share of everything they bring in, you've changed the relationship. It's still leverage, but now you have a contractor-contractee relationship.

Leverage your network, and people you know are working with you on a project that you all believe in. You're not building on their success or asking a friend to *give* you success. You're creating success and sharing it—and you're doing it with much less effort.

I've made a career out of leveraging people and assets to benefit all involved. From my humble beginnings offering free software to those who would prepare reviews for my publication to bootstrapping *The Next Internet Millionaire* reality show with friends and associates who wanted to be a part of the project, leveraging is one of my favorite concepts for fun!

THE POWER OF THE ASK

Mia Voss is a social influencer and a travel and lifestyle blogger. As her fiftieth birthday approached, she decided she wanted to do something that she'd long dreamed of doing. She wanted to spend a few weeks traveling around Italy . . . but she also didn't want to pay for the trip herself.

Leveraging gave her a solution.

First, she contacted four different influencers online. She told them that she would be traveling around Italy and asked them to share her content while she was on the road. She'd give them the tweets, the posts, and the videos, and they'd share them with their audiences. In return, she'd share their content with her followers.

She then added together all her followers and the followers of those other influencers and approached companies associated with travel. She talked to hotels, PR companies, and car firms, and she told them that in return for letting her use their services for free, she'd put their brands in front of the audiences of five different influencers.

Because Mia leveraged her connections, everyone benefited. The other influencers received good content and a bigger audience. The brands received extra reach without paying any cash. And Mia got to celebrate her fiftieth birthday traveling around Italy for three weeks for free. She had a lot of fun by inviting others to participate in this exciting endeavor. While she certainly exerted effort to make calls and do the work, it didn't feel like hustle and grind to her. Smart, right? Oh, and fun!

ENJOYING THE BLANK SPACES

One of the problems with that hustle and grind is that it's possible to put in an eleven-hour day and have far less to show for it than Mia received. A lot of the long days that I previously worked, I was just spinning wheels. It was a lot of empty activity that stole my time. But I filled those hours because I was afraid of the empty space. Even if you've made that one call at nine in the morning that closes a deal and pays the month's mortgage, you'd still feel guilty about taking the rest of the day off.

We all suffer from that guilt. We all believe the old lies about working all out all the time, even if that means missing a child's recital or not spending an evening with your spouse. And some people just work to escape. Workaholism can be a devastating addiction. It might not kill physically, but it can certainly kill a marriage. It can kill a relationship with children. It can kill a relationship with friends. It's just not healthy. But it fills the hole in the soul with hours of activity, even if that activity doesn't produce anything—and even if it does.

Putting something in a place that wasn't created for that thing makes for a bad fit. It's the square peg in the round hole. In the same way, hustle and grind can produce a false sense of accomplishment that's based on the amount of effort put in but not on the results that come out.

That's what makes leveraging such a challenge. It produces a better-quality result. It does it in less time and with less effort. And it leaves blank spaces that you can fill in any way you want. For anyone, figuring out what they want to do with that time is difficult. But for workaholics, it's terrifying.

WHAT WOULD YOUR LIFE LOOK LIKE?

It's always a worthwhile exercise to ask yourself what you would do if you had everything you were trying to accomplish. If you had money or fame or power—or all three. What would you do with your time? Sure, you'd pay off your debts and you'd take a vacation. Maybe you'd take a year off. But at some point you're going to come back, and what are you going to do with yourself then? What is your purpose?

Most people might just want to put their heads down and think that they'll figure that one out when they get there. But if you don't know what lies "there," how will you know whether you want it or how much effort it's worth to win it?

The movement from being time oriented to being outcome oriented produces a real change in the way you work. You no longer spin wheels just to keep them moving and to keep filling the hours. The empty hours aren't wasted. They're spent recharging, or being alone with your thoughts, or hanging out with a friend, or going to a concert, or sharing a meal. The autonomy that comes from the freedom to choose how we spend our lives is part of what fun is all about. It's the antidote to the hustle and grind, and it's easy to do with leveraging.

→16←

TIMING IS EVERYTHING

Patience really is a virtue. Waiting for the right time for things to take place is essential—and difficult. Finding the balance between waiting for something to happen and making something happen isn't easy.

The biggest opportunities, for example, happen through connections, but even creating those connections can take patience and timing. Introducing two people who can make things happen is rewarding and exciting, but we all have to be protective of our contacts. We have to be the gatekeepers for our friends. They've entrusted that to us. If you're asking for an introduction, you need to have already built up a relationship of trust with the person who's making the introduction.

The person you need to meet needs to be open to the opportunity you're offering at that particular time. "Not now" is a reasonable answer to an offer. I do a lot of podcast interviews, and sometimes I need to take a break from them because I get burnt out. I need to freshen up the stories. So if a request comes in, I might say: "Would love to do it. Contact me in October, and we'll get something booked for that quarter." Timing matters.

And patience matters too. Working with other people, leveraging relationships, means plenty of waiting: waiting for them to create the product, post the content, make the introduction. Push and you can break the relationship. Wait too long and it can fade away. A gentle nudge at the right moment followed by a grace period is fine. Just be human.

The good news is that patience grows. It comes with time. A twenty-five-year-old with a dream can't understand why he hasn't made it yet. A fifty-two-year-old with a dream can look back on the path that has brought him to where he is and see where he's going.

The twenties are a time to play, to experiment, to make mistakes and figure out who you are. Get fired, quit, try things. Fail. Maybe get your first big break. It's a time when no one really knows what they're doing, and it comes before the time when we know a little about what we're doing and yet still fail.

The older we get, the more we realize that we really have no clue, and we're okay with that. It's liberating. We feel confident enough to try even riskier things because we have the track record of knowing that a number of them will work out.

We might even get a home run or two in there. In time, we learn how to do things and we learn to try to do things.

A TIME TO TRY

In 2017 rapper Ja Rule tried something he'd never done before. He got together with a bunch of other people, leveraged influencers on social media, and organized a luxury music festival. It was supposed to be like Glastonbury but in the Caribbean, with fancy tents and better food and wealthy, young people.

They dreamed big, and they crashed bigger. It was a disaster. Tickets, which included plane fares, had cost from $1,000 to as much as $12,000. Instead of receiving catered food, attendees received cheese sandwiches. Instead of being housed in glamorous conditions, people were put up in what looked like a refugee camp. Bands dropped out. Festivalgoers were stranded at the airport on the way in, then stranded again on the way out. Social media was filled with pictures of the disaster. Lawsuits flew.

Ja Rule and his friends were guys with big ideas, but their execution was ineptitude of the highest order. Does that mean they shouldn't have tried? Unless their intent had always been to take the money and run, of course they should have tried! It just would have been better if they had waited until they had the skills and the experience to make something so difficult work.

Few events have crashed as badly as the Fyre Festival. For most failures, the remedy isn't lawyers and court appearances but nothing more difficult than an apology (and a refund). When you own your mistakes, people can be amazingly forgiving. When Steve Harvey read out the wrong winner at the Miss Universe contest, he came right out on stage and took full responsibility. He apologized and owned his error. That honesty not only saved, but reinforced, his career. People identified with it because we can all relate to making mistakes, and we all understand that giving in to the fear of making a mistake means that you do nothing. Your eulogy becomes: "He was born, he died, and in between he didn't really do much."

If that's the impact you want to have on the world, then don't take any risks. But if you're holding back on the gifts that you have to bring to the world out of fear, then you're doing life wrong. You're not having fun. If there's something in your heart that you want to try but you're afraid to do it, that could be a solid indicator of exactly what you ought to try. Anybody who's ever had success will tell you that they had to step outside their comfort zone—and they had to choose the moment to take that step.

When David Hancock was still a mortgage banker running a little publishing company on the side, he met Armand Morin, one of the pioneers of internet marketing. Armand was launching his first Big Seminar—the first of a series of huge internet marketing conferences—and he invited David to take part.

David knew there might be opportunities for his business over in Dallas, but he just wasn't ready. "Whatever the reasons—psychological, mental—I just wasn't there yet," he recalls. "I was still working as a banker and I was playing

IF YOU'RE HOLDING
BACK ON THE GIFTS
THAT YOU HAVE
TO BRING TO THE
WORLD OUT OF
FEAR, THEN YOU'RE
DOING LIFE WRONG.

publisher on the side. I was having a blast and doing well, but I just wasn't ready to step out."

He missed that event, but when Armand called and asked for David's help with the second event, he showed up to lend his friend a hand. David hasn't looked back since. He's made a name for himself for the vocal support he gives to speakers, and he's built a full-time, successful business providing book services for entrepreneurs.

We just have to find the right moment to take the risk and be ready to take that step—and be strong enough to cope with the new discomfort.

A TIME TO STAND STRONG

Resilience is vital. We're all born with it. We don't walk without falling down. We land on our faces. We land on our butts. We cry, but then we get up and we do it again. Only later do we learn to feel shame or embarrassment at having failed, and we have to learn to unlearn it, to ignore the pointed fingers, the laughter, the shaking heads, and the I-told-you-so's.

There are always haters in business. Jay Baer's book *Hug Your Haters* really takes a great approach to critics from a customer service perspective. People who are upset usually just need something, so the goal as a business owner is to spot that need and meet it. The passion that those people have against the business can then be turned around so that they become a raving fan. Strong emotions can swing very quickly.[1] I would rather have somebody who has an honest problem with me or with what I'm doing that can be remedied than somebody who just doesn't like me because of their own personal bias. Bad customer experiences can always be turned into good ones.

This is a different scenario from dealing with trolls, who are not responding to the business. Trolls just make your life miserable, and there's no dealing with them. On social media you can just block them—and you can do the same thing in real life. We get to decide who is in our life. We get to decide whether this person will be a customer or whether we want to show them the door. We get to create our service policy and stand by it.

There will always be people who tell you that you can't. Always. They might be too busy languishing in their own sea of not doing anything, or not being productive, or not accomplishing their goals. The schoolyard bully pushes people down in order to make himself feel bigger. You keep healthy people in your world and shut out the others. There aren't many of them, but their criticism can have an impact.

In time, though, we become immune to mean-spirited criticism. We shut it out more quickly and learn to tune in to the voices of the people who are more supportive. We learn to distinguish between helpful criticism and mean-spirited put-downs. It comes with time and experience.

A TIME TO STRIKE

If you had the opportunity to share a dinner conversation with anyone alive or dead, who would you want to dine with? This question has been asked many times, and the typical answers are Jesus, Einstein, Mozart, Trump, and so on. But my answer to this question has been one which I believe will still happen. I want to share a meal and converse with Weird Al Yankovic. Yes, you read that right. Weird Al. (Maybe someone reading this book can facilitate this epic meal?)

As a boy I used to listen to Dr. Demento's weekly show on Chicago radio, enamored with parody songs. His career launched by Demento's show, Weird Al is now a cultural icon. Not only that, but he is a shrewd businessman who leverages technology and understands his audience. The icing on the cake? He's FUN!

Inspired by Weird Al and other artists that Dr. Demento would share with his listeners, I have enjoyed dabbling with my own parody lyrics. With the success of my iFart app, I decided to connect my passions for parody, music, marketing, and fun by writing a song to the tune of Katy Perry's *Roar*. It was called *Fart*, naturally.

I wrote the lyrics, bought the license for the music, and sent somebody to the studio to record it. It came out beautifully. Best song since *Hotel California*. Okay, it wasn't the greatest piece of songwriting ever, but it was a bit of fun. It was also a year late. By the time I'd made the track, the original song had ridden through the charts and back out again. There was a time to release it, and I had missed it.

You can apply that lesson to any business. Trends come and trends go. It doesn't make as much sense to sell memorabilia for the Denver Broncos now as it did right after they had won the Super Bowl.

Some people put timing down to luck. I don't believe there's any such thing. We use the terms *luck* and *chance* to describe seemingly random events, but everything happens for a purpose. People come into our lives at the right time for a reason, but that doesn't mean that moment is the right time to strike. It takes discernment to learn when the iron is hot and when it's only warming up. It takes time and experience. High enthusiasm is not the same as good timing. It's not the same as analyzing the business opportunity and assessing whether it will work.

How many partnerships have started quickly and ended horribly? How many marriages start the same way? Love might strike at first sight, but it's the glow that follows that determines whether the relationship will avoid turning cold.

But sometimes you've just got to go for it because there's no model. There's no checklist of things to do before taking a leap. Many of the greatest successes occurred when people went off the rails, not building on a foundation but creating their own. Only in retrospect can we say that Mark Zuckerberg's decision to leave Harvard to focus on Facebook instead of completing his degree first was a good idea. He took a risk. Part of following a dream is having the courage to create your own models of action, to find your own way of doing things.

Not every trail has been blazed. Not every signpost is marked. Just because we've mapped the world doesn't mean that all the paths have been laid. The sea bed is full of treasure and sunken ships and species we haven't discovered yet. As long as there are people with big dreams and big ideas, there are new places to go—and a time to set sail.

HOW YOU DO IT CAN ALSO BE FUN

Brian Carter is doing what many people believe will make them happy. He owns his own business, The Brian Carter Group, which helps other businesses market themselves better. His clients have included some of the top fifty companies in the Fortune 500. Journalists at outlets including *The Wall Street Journal*, *US News & World Report*, ABC News, and Bloomberg TV have interviewed him to share his expertise with their audiences. IBM named him an "Influencer and Futurist," and LinkedIn placed him in its list of "Top 25 Social Media Marketing Experts You Need to Know."

When he's not using data, psychology, and creativity to help large firms motivate customers to take action, there's a good chance he'll be standing on a stage somewhere, addressing a room filled with decision makers and helping them make smart, million-dollar decisions.

That sounds like fun, and it should be. But plenty of people have been in that position and not found it fun. Just as there's no shortage of wealthy lawyers who hate their jobs and secretly wish that they'd stuck with the carpentry they enjoyed at school, so there's no shortage of business owners who have created serious, successful corporations only to feel trapped by the responsibility and the demands of what has become a J-O-B.

When that happens, you've got two choices. You can either walk away and do something else, or you can stay where you are and do what you're doing in a different way.

Spend any time with Brian Carter, and you'll soon realize that he's not the kind of guy you'd expect to find leading an important business. He's constantly cracking jokes. He'll suddenly throw out a weird voice. In the middle of a serious conversation about ad types and Facebook marketing, you'll find yourself cracking up with laughter.

That's because Brian is also a comedian. He spent two years studying screenwriting, and he still hits the comedy clubs sometimes, facing the hecklers and meeting the challenge of making a room laugh. He does that because he wants to. He enjoys it and finds it fun.

And he's also found that it's a good way to improve his creativity, making his own business both more successful and more enjoyable.

"When I started doing stand-up, it was a chance to explore new ideas," he explains. "And I read that one of the reasons people laugh is that it's a chance to build connections between two ideas that have never been connected before."

In writing jokes for audiences in comedy clubs, Brian gets to generate new concepts that he can then apply to his keynote addresses and to the campaigns he runs for his clients.

Those two aspects of Brian's nature don't always mix. "I did a keynote for a nationwide business, and it was very funny and motivating," he recalls. "Then I did a webinar for them that was incredibly serious, explaining how to tell apart buyers, non-buyers, and fans in Facebook ads and in emails. They were blown away because they thought this guy was just funny."

Sometimes the solution to an activity that isn't fun is to change the activity. But sometimes it can be simply to change the way you do that activity—and in the process, make it both more enjoyable and more successful.

→17←

THERE'S MORE TO THIS LIFE

I believe there is a plan and a purpose for our lives. We are not here by accident. Your parents may or may not have planned you, but I promise that your life is no accident. But that purpose is almost never reached in a straight line. We wiggle backward and forward and sometimes fly off on tangents as we align with the person we were meant to be. When we do, we find our greatest satisfaction in life. It's the gap between who we are and what we do that causes many of our struggles.

We all have unique passions, talents, and some innate skills. And we all have the opportunity to develop our abilities. We have a personality that comes from both our DNA and the environments that have shaped us. We each have a purpose, and we also have the opportunity to experience unexpected blessing.

Back in 1995 when I was working on my first website, I was in trouble. We had no income and had just about blown through all the angel investment. My partner had thrown in the towel and gone to work for Microsoft. I had two young kids then, one of them less than a year old.

I remember turning to my wife and saying, "I really felt that this was what I was supposed to do and it's not happening. I don't know what else to do."

So I did what anyone with absolutely no hope would do. I got down on my knees and prayed. It wasn't one of those stoic prayers either. I think it was more of a primal scream that sounded like "HEEEEEEEEEEEELP!"

There's something to be said for humility, for just making yourself vulnerable and accepting your position. I had sold encyclopedias before, so I went back to the regional office and talked to the manager. Even as I was there, I was thinking, "I don't belong here. This isn't where I'm meant to be." Perhaps it's true what they say. You can never go back.

A week later, when we were down to less than two dollars in our checking account, I received an email from a gentleman in Washington state. He claimed to represent a Japanese multimedia conglomerate that was interested in licensing content on my site and localizing it. I'd never heard of this man, nor the company he claimed to represent, called Takarajimasha. Go ahead, you try and pronounce it!

As he was talking to me, I was thinking that this deal was

probably worth a couple hundred bucks. But I'd learned from sales that you don't open your mouth when someone else is talking. So before I knew it, he was detailing their proposal: they wanted to pay me $5,000 a month to license my content. That was enough to solve all our financial problems.

Now, I didn't know this guy. I couldn't have solicited this guy. I never would have thought of licensing content, and especially not to Japan. But the deal ended up being worth $7,500 a month for eighteen months. It fell out of the sky.

Some people might just say that I was lucky, but I really think that when we're following the path that we believe we're supposed to be on, we're going to encounter resistance. We're going to hit obstacles that will cause us to question if we're doing the right thing. Those obstacles will test our faith. We'll have moments of humility in which we need to ask for help. And sometimes that help will arrive in the most unusual and unexpected ways.

When you see that help arrive, you can't help but feel that it could happen again. It breeds faith. Faith grows when it's watered, and it's watered every time something happens that feels like an invisible hand leading you down the road. I've experienced it many times in my life: a call out of the blue, a chance encounter that transforms my business, an idea that just hits. I think it's part of a design. You can call it luck if you want, but whether it's just good fortune or a glimpse at your life's road map, you've still got to use it.

There's a story that's been shared many times, many different ways. I happen to like the one about a guy hanging off a cliff. He's dangling by one arm, and he prays to God to save him. A man appears at the top of the cliff. He sees the guy hanging there, and he says: "Hold on! I'll get help."

The guy looks up and says: "It's okay. I'm fine. God will save me."

The fire service turns up, but before they can roll out the ladder, the guy calls down and says: "It's okay. I'm fine. God will save me."

Then a helicopter appears overhead, and when the rescuer drops down the rope and reaches for the man's spare hand, the man looks up and says, "It's okay. I'm fine. God will save me."

Then a voice booms out from the heavens, "I sent a guy. I sent the fire service. I sent a helicopter. What more do you want?"

We receive help all the time. We're blessed and fortunate all the time. Our job is to recognize those blessings, humbly receive them, and express sincere gratitude that we're not in this alone.

THERE'S MORE TO MURPHY

Faith is not *hoping* that something will happen. It's a true, deep sense that something *will* happen, even if you can't explain it.

It's like boarding an airplane, believing that you're going to fly at thirty-six thousand feet and land at the destination marked on your ticket. You know you're going to get there even though you don't understand aerodynamics. You might have a vague awareness that air passing over wings creates lift, but how it does it and how it manages to lift several tons of steel and passengers up into the air, keep them there, and bring them down safely at exactly the right spot on the world? That feels like a miracle. It feels like faith.

We trust good results to happen even when we don't know how they can happen. It's the opposite of Murphy's Law. As I said earlier, I don't believe things always go wrong, but I am pretty certain that they never go the way you think they will. Expect the unexpected at every turn, and you're rarely surprised.

I've had several seasons of business during which things went really well. That eighteen-month contract with the Japanese company was supposed to have lasted three years, but they changed their model and it was cut short. AdSense revenue can flow in in huge amounts, only for Google to change something in its algorithm and everything dries up.

It's human nature to worry. We spend countless hours that turn collectively into days, weeks, months, and maybe even years of anxiety and fear about things that usually never happen. It's a huge waste of energy and time. The more faith we have and the more faith we exercise, the less we worry. Just as we learn patience when we exercise patience, so faith grows the more we use it. When something is going well, it's tempting to think it's always going to be like that. Experience teaches us to prepare for change. Faith teaches us that that change will eventually be for the best and gives us the strength to use those new opportunities so that we don't miss them when they arrive.

EXPECT THE UNEXPECTED AT EVERY TURN, AND YOU'RE RARELY SURPRISED.

LOOKING BACK

People often realize too late that there's more to this life. The later we realize it, the greater the regrets, and regret is a horrible thing. We all have regrets. We've all done something we wish we hadn't. But I don't think anybody ever looks back and says: "I had too much fun. I enjoyed my life too much. I enjoyed what I was doing, and I enjoyed the people I was with. I should have spent more time in the office."

Minimizing those regrets requires action. The worst regret is to have never tried, to have never attempted to reach what you hunger for. Of course, there are times when those goals feel out of reach. There are always times when we fall back or fall down and struggle to rise again. There's a time for grieving, for recuperation, for rebuilding. Sometimes we have to formulate new dreams and new hopes based on our new circumstances. We have to ask ourselves, what *can* we do if we can't do that? What were we meant to do if it wasn't what we thought?

In the end, we have to meet those three basic needs: to experience love, to belong, and to feel significant. The most self-actualized people are those who reach the end of their lives and say, "I was loved and I loved. I belonged and found my place. I impacted others' lives."

⇥18⇤

BABY STEPS TO THE BOAT

I f you take away just one idea from this book, I hope it's that you have to start somewhere. You have to take the first steps toward living with fun.

Those steps can be small. They can be tiny. But they add up.

What About Bob is one of my favorite films. Bill Murray is absolutely brilliant as an obsessive-compulsive neurotic who makes his therapist (played by Richard Dreyfuss) absolutely batty by invading his family vacation at Lake Winnipesaukee.

Before everything goes awry, Dr. Leo Marvin (Dreyfuss) suggests Bob Wiley (Murray) read his new best-selling book, *Baby Steps*, in order to help Bob deal with his neurosis while the therapist is away on vacation.

Bob takes the baby steps quite literally in the beginning, shuffling his feet quite slowly out the door, down the stairs, and to his vehicle. But once at the lake with the doctor and his family, Bob sees an opportunity to overcome his fear of the water by baby-stepping to the boat. If you've seen the film, you'll smirk at this quote: "I'm sailing!" If not, put it on your must-see list.[1]

The point is that sometimes baby steps can be more impactful than large strides.

After the Second World War, Japan was in ruins. Two of its most important industrial cities had been turned into radio-active wastelands. Its cities were ashes. It had lost millions of people and was under foreign occupation. Within twenty-five years, it had grown into one of the world's largest economies, second only to the United States.

There were all sorts of reasons for that rapid growth, but one of them was the philosophy of *kaizen*, or continual improvement. Each day you do a little better, align yourself a little more closely, take another step closer to where you want to go.

Those small steps build. They compound so that one small improvement on the first day becomes a giant leap with the same effort a month later. It's like doubling your money every day. On the first day, you receive a penny. On the second day, you get two. On the third day, four cents, and so on. After a week, you'd receive just 64 cents. But after sixteen days, you'd be getting over $327, and after thirty days, you'd receive $5.36 million.

Results don't double in quite the same way, but action

SOMETIMES BABY STEPS CAN BE MORE IMPACTFUL THAN LARGE STRIDES.

does have a compound effect. As you develop the confidence to do something that you connect with, that you enjoy doing, you experience the excitement, the thrill, and the exhilaration of doing something new. Even if it looked hard. Even if it looked scary. The enjoyment gives you the confidence to do it again or try something else. And every time you take that step, that single, small step, you start walking. Those steps become strides, which turn into running, then leaping over hurdles, and finally jumping tall buildings.

It doesn't happen immediately. You don't move from a job you don't like to a life you love overnight. Everything happens in its own time. Plant a seed in the ground, and you won't wake up the following morning to find a tree. That's not how it works. That seed has to take root in the soil. It has to slowly push out that first bud. It has to roll out a leaf to catch the sun, and once it's able to use the sun's energy instead of just the energy in the seed, it's able to grow a little faster. It can push out another leaf and absorb twice the amount of energy, and so on. And all the time it's growing, it needs water. It needs care and the proper environment.

We're no different. To grow into the people we're meant to be, we have to put ourselves in the right situation, meet the right people, be in the right places, take risks, and take action at the right time without forcing it. We have to trust that good stuff will come when we put our own good stuff out there.

We have to have integrity and honor because what goes around comes around. I've seen plenty of people who have taken advantage of others, burned their bridges, and struggle to get anybody to work with them. They demonstrated through their actions that they were not trustworthy.

In the end, life is too short for that. Whether you believe that man has walked the earth for six or seven millennia or a few million years in different forms, our life span, as long as it is right now, is still a blip. We have a short time to make an impact, to suck the marrow out of every day in a way that causes us to be nourished and grow so that we can pour out to others.

Have fun, and share your gifts. You need to live with fun, and the world wants to live with your joy.

OFFER FOR THE READER

ARE YOU READY TO
IMPLEMENT *THE FUN FORMULA?*

Get instant access to Joel's **FREE Fun Formula checklist!**
Featuring key action items from this book, this downloadable
checklist will help you fast track and fine-tune your direction in
business and life. Small adjustments can have a massive ripple
effect on bringing you the joy and fulfillment you seek. Grab
this checklist now and get started.

Go to FunFormulaBook.com/checklist

ACKNOWLEDGMENTS

Fun is more than a journey. It's a journey that most often takes place because of, and along with, others. Without those who have poured into my life and who have permitted me to pour back into their lives, Fun just wouldn't be as much fun.

I could undoubtedly fill several pages of those who fit into one of these categories, but I want to put the spotlight on just a few who have walked alongside me on the journey of this book, the title that I consider my "core" message.

To my agent, Bruce Barbour, who instantly got behind the idea for this book and successfully brought it to just the right publishing house.

To Webster Younce, associate publisher at Thomas Nelson, and his support team: thanks for being a great partner and believing in this message.

To all the guests of the *Fun with Joel Comm Podcast*: many of your stories made it into this manuscript. You are living, breathing examples of Fun and I'm grateful to know each of you.

To Brenton Weyi, for patiently asking great questions as I recorded the stories and concepts for each chapter. You helped me thoroughly distill my ideas to core concepts that I believe are universally applicable.

To my kids, Zach and Jenna, who always bring fun into my heart. I love you both so much!

And finally, to my friends who are always fun to be around. We've got the "adulting" thing figured out, but this "growing up" concept is just never going to find a home in our souls. Thank you, Erin, Ken, Lou, BK, EBR, Mikey, Ward, Ray, Sammy, David, Kimberly, Dan, Beaner, Teedubs, and so many others. You rock!

ABOUT THE AUTHOR

Joel Comm is a *New York Times* bestselling author, professional keynote speaker, social media marketing strategist, live video expert, technologist, brand influencer, futurist, and eternal twelve-year-old. With more than two decades of experience harnessing the power of the web, publishing, social media, and mobile applications to expand reach and engage in active relationship marketing, Joel is a sought-after public speaker who leaves his audiences inspired, entertained, and armed with strategic tools to create highly effective new media campaigns. His latest serendipitous project is as cohost of the *Bad Crypto Podcast*, a top cryptocurrency show making the future of digital payments easy for others to understand.

NOTES

Chapter 1: How Did We Get Here?

1. "2013 Teens & Career Survey Executive Summary," Juniorachievement.org, https://www.juniorachievement.org/web/ja-usa/ja-in-the-news/-/blogs/2013-teens-careers-survey/.
2. *Oxford Dictionaries*, s.v. "play," accessed October 20, 2017, https://en.oxforddictionaries.com/definition/play.
3. "Gap Year Data & Benefits," American Gap Association, accessed October 20, 2017, https://americangap.org/data-benefits.php.
4. Nina Hoe, "American Gap Association National Alumni Survey Report," 2015, http://americangap.org/assets/2015%20NAS%20Report.pdf, 11.
5. Bronnie Ware, *The Top Five Regrets of the Dying* (Carlsbad, CA: Hay House, 2012).

Chapter 3: What Does Fun Even Mean?

1. Andrew Anthony, "Why the Secret to Productivity Isn't Longer Hours," *The Guardian*, January 22, 2017, https://www.theguardian.com/money/2017/jan/22/alex-soojung-kim-pang-interview-rest-why-you-get-more-done-when-you-work-less.

2. Alex Soojung-Kim Pang, *Rest: Why You Get More Done When You Work Less* (New York: Basic Books, 2016), introduction.

3. Pang, *Rest*, loc. 761 of 4679, Kindle.

Chapter 4: Who Am I?

1. Tim Ferriss, *Tools of Titans* (New York: Houghton Mifflin Harcourt, 2017), 309–12.

Chapter 6: Keeping It Real

1. Chenkai Wu, Michelle C. Odden, Gwenith G. Fisher, and Robert S. Stawski, "Association of Retirement Age with Mortality: A Population-Based Longitudinal Study Among Older Adults in the USA," *Journal of Epidemiology and Community Health*, March 21, 2016, doi: 10.1136/jech-2015-207097.

Chapter 8: Work and Play Are Made to Go Together

1. Bill Snyder, "Debra Lee: 'Work Should Be Fun'," Insights by Stanford Business, March 24, 2017, https://www.gsb.stanford.edu/insights/debra-lee-work-should-be-fun.

Chapter 9: Hobbies Can Become a Career—and Often Do

1. Tim Urban, "The Tail End," *Wait But Why* (blog), December 11, 2015, https://waitbutwhy.com/2015/12/the-tail-end.html.

2. Jaruwan Sakulku and James Alexander, "The Impostor Phenomenon," *International Journal of Behavioral Science* 6, no. 1 (2011): 75–97.

Chapter 10: Choose Your Friends Wisely

1. Henry Cloud and John Townsend, *Boundaries: When to Say Yes, How to Say No to Take Control of Your Life* (Grand Rapids, MI: Zondervan, 1992), 29–30.

2. Ellen Langer, Arthur Blank, and Benzion Chanowitz, "The Mindlessness of Ostensibly Thoughtful Action: The Role of 'Placebic' Information in Interpersonal Interaction," *Journal of*

Personality and Social Psychology, 36, no. 6 (1978): 635–42, http://citeseerx.ist.psu.edu/viewdoc/download?doi =10.1.1.318.1028&rep=rep1&type=pdf.

3. Terry Cole-Whittaker, *What You Think of Me Is None of My Business* (New York: Berkley, 1979).

Chapter 11: Hooray for Failure

1. Chris Beier, "How ClassPass Got the Product Wrong Twice Before It Was Right," *Inc.* Video, 3:53, accessed October 26, 2017, https://www.inc.com/payal-kadakia/how-classpass-got-the-product-wrong-twice-before-it-was-right.html.

2. Polina Marinova, "ClassPass Founder Payal Kadakia Is Stepping Down as CEO," *Fortune,* March 17, 2017, http://fortune.com/2017/03/17/classpass-payal-kadakia-ceo/.

Chapter 12: Be Willing to Shift

1. Neil Gaiman, "Gaiman on Copyright Piracy and the Web," YouTube, 4:20, published by Open Rights Group, February 3, 2011, https://www.youtube.com/watch?v=0Qkyt1wXNlI.

Chapter 14: The Hustle Is a Dance and Grinding Is for Coffee Beans

1. Yalda T. Uhls and Patricia Greenfield, "The Value of Fame: Preadolescent Perceptions of Popular Media and Their Relationship to Future Aspirations," *Developmental Psychology,* December 19, 2011, http://www.cdmc.ucla.edu/Welcome_files/The%20value%20of%20fame-1.pdf.

2. Mark Schaefer, *Known: The Handbook for Building and Unleashing Your Personal Brand in the Digital Age* (Louisville, KY: Schaefer Marketing Solutions, 2017).

3. William B. Strean, "Laughter Prescription," *College of Family Physicians of Canada* 55, no. 10 (October 2009): 965–67, https://www.ncbi.nlm.nih.gov/pmc/articles/PMC2762283/.

Chapter 16: Timing Is Everything

1. Jay Baer, *Hug Your Haters: How to Embrace Complaints and Keep Your Customers* (New York: Portfolio, 2016).

Chapter 18: Baby Steps to the Boat

1. Alvin Sargent, Laura Ziskin, and Tom Schulman, *What About Bob?* directed by Frank Oz (Burbank, CA: Touchstone Pictures, 1991).